SCHOOL LIBRARIANSHIP SERIES
Edited by Diane de Cordova Biesel

1. *Reference Work in School Library Media Centers: A Book of Case Studies*, by Amy G. Job and MaryKay W. Schnare, 1996.
2. *The School Library Media Specialist as Manager: A Book of Case Studies*, by Amy G. Job and MaryKay W. Schnare, 1997.
3. *Forecasting the Future: School Media Programs in an Age of Change*, by Kieth C. Wright and Judith F. Davie, 1999.
4. *Now What Do I Do?: Things They Never Taught in Library School—A Book of Case Studies,* by Amy G. Job and MaryKay W. Schnare, 2001.

Now What Do I Do?

Things They Never Taught in Library School—A Book of Case Studies

Amy G. Job
MaryKay W. Schnare

School Librarianship Series No. 4

The Scarecrow Press, Inc.
Lanham, Maryland, and London
2001

SCARECROW PRESS, INC.

Published in the United States of America
by Scarecrow Press, Inc.
4720 Boston Way, Lanham, Maryland 20706
www.scarecrowpress.com

4 Pleydell Gardens, Folkestone
Kent CT20 2DN, England

Copyright © 2001 by Amy G. Job and MaryKay W. Schnare

All rights reserved. No part of this publication may be reproduced, stored in a retrieval system, or transmitted in any form or by any means, electronic, mechanical, photocopying, recording, or otherwise, without the prior permission of the publisher.

British Library Cataloguing in Publication Information Available

Library of Congress Cataloging-in-Publication Data
Job, Amy G.
    Now what do I do? : things they never taught in library school / Amy G. Job, MaryKay Schnare.
     p. cm. — (School Librarianship series ; no. 4)
    Includes bibliographical references.
    ISBN 0-8108-3990-3 (alk. paper) — ISBN 0-8108-3991-1 (pbk. : alk. paper)
     1. School libraries—United States—Administration—Case studies. 2. Instructional materials centers—United States—Administration—Case studies. 3. School libraries—United States—Administration. 4. Instructional materials centers—United States—Administration. I. Schnare, MaryKay, 1945- II. Title. III. Series.

Z675.S3 J59 2001
025.1'978'0973—dc21

00-067056

∞™ The paper used in this publication meets the minimum requirements of American National Standard for Information Sciences—Permanence of Paper for Printed Library Materials, ANSI/NISO Z39.48-1992.
Manufactured in the United States of America.

Contents

Foreword		ix
Introduction		xi

Part I. Nitty Gritty: Emergencies, etc.

1	Medical	3
	Michael's Fit	3
	Books and Suicide	4
	The Labor Question	6
	Shooting Stars	7
	The Liquor Case	9
2	Physical Plant	11
	The Leak from on High	11
	Displays Everywhere	12
	Vandalism Here, There, and Everywhere	14
	Micey, Micey!	17
3	Personal	21
	Crushes	21
	There All the Time	23
	Here They Come!	25
	Stories, Stories, Stories	28
	Smoking in the Boys' Room	30
	Is This Discrimination?	32
4	Personnel	35
	After Hours and the Union	35
	I Dare You!	38
	Go Sit in the Corner	40
	Where Is Larry?	42

vi Contents

        The Library Media Center as Punishment Room   44
        The Library Media Specialist Is Also the Nurse?   46
5 Potholes on the Information Highway   51
        Cataloging Electronic/Internet Resources   51
        Roasted Computers   53
        The Hacker   55
        It Is All Part of the Job—Or Is It?   57
        Who Is Minding the Students in the Lab?   59
        Smut in the Middle School   62
        The District Cut Out the Magazines   64

**Part II. Bigger Issues:
Planning, Policies, and Personnel**

6 Certification   71
        Paraprofessional Volunteers   71
        Here Comes the Supervisor   73
        The Big Re-Licensing Issue   75
        Emergency Certification   77
        Grow Your Own School Library Media Specialist   79
        Emergency Certificate = Harassment?   83
7 Policies   87
        Filters, Filters, Filters   87
        Money, Money, Money—Just Not Enough, Just Not
           Where It Is Needed   89
        I Thought That Sharing Was a Good Thing   92
        Get That Filthy Book Out of Here!   95
        I Didn't Borrow the Books from the Public Library,
           so Why Should I Worry if They Are Missing?   98
        I Am Sure That I Paid for That   101
        Selling to Children—Right, Wrong, Legal?   104
8 Personnel   109
        Managing from Afar, or Butting in Where You Don't
           Belong?   109
        Let Them Learn Alphabetical Order   111
        Who Pays for Professional Development?   114
        Caught in the Middle   117
        The Substitute Expert   120

9	Scheduling	123
	Here He Is—Super Library Media Specialist!	123
	And She Just Keeps Rollin' Along	126
	Fixed to Be Flexible—You Do It	128
10	Physical Plant	131
	Moving Day	131
	Our Beautiful New School Library Media Center	133
	Close the Library Media Center—I Need More Classroom Space	135
	Closing the Library Media Center Again!	137

Part III. Appendices

A.	AASL Position Statement on Access to Resources	143
B.	AASL Position Paper on Information Literacy	145
C.	AASL Position Paper on Appropriate Staffing	155
D.	AASL Position Statement on Flexible Scheduling	157
E.	AASL Position Statement on Preparation of School Library Media Specialists	159
F.	AASL Position Statement on Resource-Based Instruction	161
G.	AASL Position Statement on the Role of the Library Media Specialist in Outcomes-Based Instruction	163
H.	AASL Position Statement on the Value of Library Media Programs in Education	167
I.	Sample Library Media Selection Policy	169
J.	Sample Library Media Policy for Reevaluation of Selected Materials	173

Bibliography	179
Periodicals	179
Books	179
Sources from the Internet	186
Suggested Readings	189
Index	191
About the Authors	193

Foreword

The works in the School Librarianship Series are directed toward the library school professor, the library school student, and the district supervisor. Each volume examines the role of the school library media specialist as an agent of change within the educational system, with the goal of exploring the philosophical basis of school librarianship yesterday, today, and tomorrow.

It has been bruited about the neighborhood some things are just not taught in most library schools. Comments concerning this perceived need revolve around crises related to health, physical safety, and the manner in which school librarians should cope with these difficulties in a compassionate and legal manner.

In the fourth book in this series, Job and Schnare have crafted some brilliant case studies that cover, among other things, the student who goes into labor, the teacher who smokes pot, and mice in the utility closet. Each case study is followed by thought-provoking questions that can be used in a variety of settings, such as a conference or a graduate school classroom. Well-written and concise, this book brings us all closer to the goal of reality.

Diane de Cordova Biesel
Series Editor

Introduction

"What do I do now?" "How do I handle this situation, or what do I do for that student?" How many times have you or someone you know asked these questions? In some cases, it might be every day; in others, occasionally. You might think to yourself that you went through a library or educational media curriculum in school, but even that isn't always sufficient to cover all of the situations that arise in a school setting. Various incidents pop up and confront you when you least expect them. Reacting to them is often difficult or overwhelming.

Knowing this from real-life situations that they, themselves, have encountered, the authors of this book have prepared a series of case studies that describes problems and poses questions that can be used by educational media students or professional-development workshops. The case situations fall outside of the subject matter of traditional library media curriculums and include topics on the "nitty gritty" issues (emergencies, etc.) and on bigger issues, such as planning, policies, and personnel. Incorporated within the cases are the concepts on information literacy found in the guide *Information Power: Building Partnerships for Learning,* issued by the American Association of School Librarians in 1998.

In a departure from the first two books of case studies in this series, the cases are arranged by topic, rather than by school level, such as elementary, middle, or secondary. Appendices consist of some of the documents included in the previous works, plus a greatly expanded bibliography of print and Internet resources. The bibliography, it is hoped, will prove to be a base for a professional collection that leads to answers to the expected, as well as the unexpected, situations that arise in the functioning of the modern school library media center.

I

NITTY GRITTY: EMERGENCIES, ETC.

• *1* •

Medical

MICHAEL'S FIT

Michael O'Brien had been a regular user of the school library media center during his years as a student in Memorial High School. He was a quiet boy who didn't mingle much with the other student groups in the school and participated in few activities. Sylvia Waterman, the school library media specialist, noticed that Michael took medication and that he had a medical alert bracelet on his wrist. She didn't think much about the significance of these signals and just considered Michael one of the quiet ones who didn't cause trouble.

Sylvia had enough to do in coping with the students who caused disruptions during her lessons and the student free-reading periods. Talking and walking around in the library media center, the unruly students refused to be considerate of others who wanted to learn and thus were often banished from the premises.

It came as a shock to Sylvia when, one day, Michael suddenly uttered a series of grunts and other unintelligible sounds, fell from his seat to the floor, and began to thrash around. It seemed as if he had decided to join the disrupters and add his special methods of annoyance. Sylvia called his name and there was no response. The other students stopped talking and stared at Michael. Then, one of the students in the class called out that it appeared that Michael was having a fit similar to the ones that her sister often had: an epileptic seizure. Sylvia hesitated for a minute and then recalled the medical bracelet on Michael's wrist. She bent over Michael and seized his arm to look at the tag. Sure enough, it indicated that Michael was subject to epileptic fits and was under medication to control his condition.

4   Chapter 1

Questions

1. What should Sylvia do next? Should the school nurse be called? Should she search his pockets to locate his medication to check on his dosage schedules? What are the proper procedures for handling epileptic patients?
2. What should Sylvia do with the rest of the class members? Many of them appeared to be in shock after viewing Michael's frantic gyrations.
3. Should Sylvia have checked before this with the school authorities about the significance of the medical bracelet and medication? Perhaps if Sylvia had known of Michael's condition, she could have watched for signals that indicated an imminent attack.

BOOKS AND SUICIDE

For as long as she could remember, Cordellia (Corky) was popular with her classmates, had parents who pampered her and gave her anything she asked for, and was an excellent student with dreams of college and a career. She was active in school activities and was editor of the school newspaper. It appeared that life was going Corky's way.

An avid reader, Corky was a frequent user of the school library media center. She knew how to use the online catalog and was able to retrieve information with little help from Ralph, the school library media specialist.

The school library media center was automated but did not have a self-checkout circulation system. The possibilities of obtaining one of those special systems had been investigated by Ralph, but due to fiscal limitations and other logistical considerations, it was felt that the self-check system was not feasible for a number of years to come.

That decision, it turned out, was fortuitous. Ralph was at the desk the day that Corky brought the books she had selected to be charged out. Ralph quickly scanned the titles and noticed that all five volumes dealt with the topic of suicide. Ralph had not heard of any assignments dealing with suicide at the weekly faculty meeting, where teachers shared their study areas with him as a planning guide. Ralph hid his shocked reaction and casually asked Corky if she was working on a paper and needed any further research materials. She quickly and, he thought, rather furtively responded that she just wanted to read the books and needed no help from him. She picked up the stamped books and left the library media center.

That conversation was on Ralph's mind for the rest of the day. He had a nagging feeling that something was wrong with Corky, and he finally decided that he needed to do something about his suspicions. He stopped at the main office on his way out, but the school nurse and guidance counselor had left for the day, and the principal and vice principal were both in meetings. Ralph decided to take matters into his own hands and used the office phone to call Corky's home. Corky's mother answered and, in response to Ralph's question, told him that Corky was not home yet and was probably in the school gym with the cheerleaders.

When Ralph arrived at the gym, he was greeted by Janice, the gym teacher. As Ralph voiced his concern, Janice suddenly remarked that she hadn't seen Corky for the past half hour and that during the preliminary practice session Corky had seemed preoccupied. Janice and Ralph immediately set off to find her, and as Janice entered the locker room, she found Corky sitting on a bench, surrounded by the books, and holding a rope with a noose in her hand. She appeared ready to throw the rope over the pipes in the ceiling. Calling Corky's name, Janice was able to distract the student and retrieve the rope.

Questions

1. What should Ralph and Janice do next? What are the legal ramifications of their actions, if any?
2. Was it proper for Ralph to call Corky's home?
3. Was it proper for Ralph to look at the titles Corky had selected for circulation and to question her on them? Is that censorship?
4. It was probably Corky's manner when she answered his question about the assignment that aroused Ralph's suspicions. Should he have acted sooner? Is this "sixth sense" a good and necessary quality for a school library media specialist to have?

THE LABOR QUESTION

Nadine hadn't looked pregnant until she was into her sixth month. She participated in after-school activities, maintained her excellent academic record, and associated with the same group of students who had been her companions all through high school—her life appeared to be like that of any other teenager in Memorial High. Memorial High School was located in the center of a suburban community of moderate- and upper-income families. The majority of the students in the school were high achievers who received an excellent pre-college education from the faculty and staff members.

It came as quite a shock to the school and local community when it was disclosed that Nadine was pregnant. Students' rights were discussed, and after lengthy deliberations the school board ruled that Nadine could remain in school as long she was physically able to and her presence did not disturb the other students in her classes.

During her final month of pregnancy, however, an incident occurred that upset the entire school, and Marcy in particular. Marcy was the school library media specialist who on that day was talking to the class of junior history students about the research tools that were available in the library media center. She had just completed a demonstration of several CD-ROM databases and was about to talk about the online catalog as a research guide. All during the class session Nadine had squirmed around in her chair at the table, and she suddenly took a deep breath and had a pained expression on her face. As she exhaled, she raised her hand and announced that she thought she was going into labor. As she spoke the words, the result on the class was electrifying. Pandemonium broke out, and soon the room was filled with shouts and screams as students rushed around, some exiting the library media center, some hovering around Nadine, and some walking around in a general panic.

Marcy attempted to outshout the students, asking them to be quiet and allow Nadine some breathing room. She went to her desk and took her bell out of the drawer and rang it. The piercing sound cut through the racket in the room and the students gradually quieted down. Nadine lay on the floor, breathing deeply and issuing occasional moans. Two of the girls in the class placed a sweater-covered book under her head and attempted to calm Nadine down.

Then Marcy went to the call box and announced that they needed immediate medical help in the library media center. Shortly thereafter, the school nurse and the principal arrived and took control. Marcy was shaken by the experience and was standing in the room, wringing her hands.

Questions

1. Did Marcy do the correct thing following Nadine's announcement? It almost appeared that Marcy was more concerned about the turmoil the students were creating than about caring for Nadine.
2. Did it appear that the school community was prepared for Nadine's sudden change? Should she have been allowed to remain in school until the very last minute? Shouldn't the school have monitored Nadine's condition?
3. How far does the concept of students' rights go? Are there any legal implications involved in this case?
4. Should Nadine and/or her parents have monitored Nadine's condition?

SHOOTING STARS

It had been a long, hard week at Lincoln Junior High School. Classes had only been in session for three weeks since the opening of the school year, and already a number of incidents had occurred, involving student vandalism, classroom disruptions, and several out-and-out fist fights. Lincoln was located in the heart of the city and had a student body that was highly transitory and often inflammatory.

The staff at Lincoln Junior High was dedicated to helping students who came from broken homes, multilingual families, and dysfunctional living environments. Staff members had a reputation for caring and concern, despite the obstacles that faced them every day.

The school did have a library media center, albeit a rather old and ill-equipped one. José did his best to provide the students with a quiet place outside the classroom for study and research. The shelves in the center were adequately stocked, but there were no automated resources and few nonprint materials. Magazines were stolen almost as soon as they were placed on the racks. The room was poorly arranged, with a number of low visibility areas. José had placed a few posters on the walls, but they were quite faded and rather decrepit in appearance.

José had dreams of a magical influx of money that would provide more resources, a better layout of the room, noise control, and all the other good things that make for an efficiently functioning library media center. It was into this dream world that José escaped, sitting at his desk, late on Friday afternoon after school officially closed. He was meditating on a pleasant future when he heard a strange shuffling noise coming from the back area of the library media center.

It was impossible to see the source of the sounds from his seat since his line of sight was blocked by a set of shelves. José reluctantly roused himself and walked around the bookcases. What he saw practically took his breath away. Sitting in the corner, in an almost fetal position, was a student who appeared to be asleep. José was surprised to see the student, who apparently had never heard the school dismissal buzzer and was ready to camp out for the night. As José approached the student, he suddenly noticed the needle on the floor by the young man's knee and the band around his arm. No sounds came from the student's mouth, and he appeared almost comatose. José came closer and lightly tapped the young man on the shoulder. There was no response. José then shook the student, and still no response. Now in a panic, José ran to the front of the library media center and down to the office where the principal was talking to a parent. José interrupted the conversation and informed the principal that he thought there was a dead student in the library media center. Upon hearing this, the principal shouted for the security guard and ran with José back to the site of the "dead" student. The shocked parent was left sitting in the office.

The security guard met José and the principal in the library media center, and José showed them both where the body was located. The guard felt for a pulse and announced that the student was not dead, merely in a drug-induced stupor.

Questions

1. What should happen next? What kind of help should be summoned?
2. Did José follow proper procedures? Should he have felt for a pulse before panicking and calling for help?
3. Is it proper or legal for a member of the school staff to touch a student under those circumstances?
4. Apparently, part of the problem was caused by the fact that the location the student had selected for his drug activities was not visible from the desk. Should José rearrange or make plans for increasing visibility for all areas?
5. It appears that José does not have much of an emergency plan in place for the library media center. What elements should be included in such a plan?

THE LIQUOR CASE

It was 9:15 in the morning and most of the students in the Pearl Miller Middle School were settled into a learning mode. The hallways were virtually deserted, except for the occasional student who went to the restrooms or to the library media center. Sandy Byrne was the library media specialist, and she was providing library instruction on science research to Holly Bargiel's class.

Sandy was working with small groups of students, helping them find biology information, when she was approached by one of the young men in the class. He asked for a pass to the boy's room and Sandy gave him the permission. She did not notice the small bulge in Chernoh's pocket when he spoke to her. He left the library media center, and Sandy mentally noted the time: 9:20 A.M.

Class time ended as the buzzer rang and students picked up their books and notebooks. They passed quickly from the room, carrying on conversations in low voices. Sandy walked around the room, pushing in chairs at the tables and picking up stray pieces of paper. When she came to Chernoh's place, she noticed that his books were still lying on the table. She realized that she had not seen Chernoh return to the library media center since he had left fifteen minutes earlier.

Sandy was just about to push the button on the intercom to inquire about Chernoh when he came through the door. She pulled her hand away from the button and asked Chernoh where he had been. He mumbled something about not feeling well, and Sandy expressed concern and asked him to pick up his papers and go to the nurse's office. Then she smelled it—the odor of liquor on Chernoh's breath.

Sandy's concern quickly changed to anger, and she reproached Chernoh for this infraction of the rules. A silly grin came over Chernoh's face, and he sat down at the table by his books. Just then the door opened, and the next class began to file into the library media center. Chernoh just sat there as the students flowed around him. Sandy ordered Chernoh to leave the library media center, but he remained sitting. Sandy wondered what to do next. If she called on the intercom, the entire class would hear her. If she did nothing, Chernoh might cause a fuss or fall asleep. It was a difficult dilemma.

Questions

1. What should Sandy have done?
2. Could she have enlisted the aid of the teacher of the incoming class?
3. Were her concerns about her lack of action valid, or should she have done something and let the pieces fall where they may?

• 2 •

Physical Plant

THE LEAK FROM ON HIGH

The date was October 23, and it was a day that Kwaku Armah would never forget. That was the day when the big storm swept over the city, causing destruction to many buildings. Electrical power was cut for several hours, but since the storm passed over during the daytime, the loss of power—though annoying because the computers, elevators, and other electrically driven machines were not able to function—had not caused a major panic.

Kwaku was the library media specialist at the Ridge Elementary School, and he had just returned from lunch when the storm hit. The power went off, and Kwaku was thankful that the computers were protected by surge protectors. Kwaku could hear the rain beating against the windows and the wind whipping around the corner of the building where the library media center was located. And then he began to hear a dripping sound that appeared to come from the shelving area in the far corner. Kwaku quickly walked over to that area and saw a horrifying sight. Water was dripping from the ceiling to the floor, and some of it was falling onto the bookshelves. Kwaku quickly grabbed several wastebaskets and placed them on the carpeting under the main drips. His next concern was the damage to the books on the shelves. He looked around the library media center and didn't see anything that could be used to cover the books. He went to the intercom and called the office, requesting that the custodian supply him with sheets of plastic. Someone in the office acknowledged his call, and Kwaku heard a call over the loudspeaker system for the custodian to go to the library media center.

12   Chapter 2

Kwaku then pulled over some empty book trucks and began to remove the water-soaked books from the shelves and place them on the trucks. By that time, the custodian arrived with the plastic and began to cover the shelves with the film. That operation was just about completed when Kwaku heard that terrible dripping sound coming from another area of the library media center.

He went over to investigate and discovered that the leak from the ceiling was falling onto the computers, the printers, and the printer paper stock. This could potentially be even worse than the wet books. Kwaku shouted for the custodian to hurry over to the computer area with his plastic sheeting. For a minute, Kwaku contemplated moving the computers and ancillary equipment, but he quickly realized that all the wires would need to be disconnected first, and there was no time for that. He helped the custodian place the plastic over the computers, but there was not enough to cover the entire computer area. The custodian left the room to retrieve some more plastic, but Kwaku realized that the damage in large part was already done. What was he to do?

Questions

1. Did Kwaku follow the proper, most expeditious procedures once he realized what had happened? Should he have attended to the books before worrying about the floor?
2. What should his next step be in handling the water-damaged books?
3. Can anything be done about the computers once they are covered with water? Even with surge protectors, is there danger of electrical shock from water and electricity once the power comes back on?
4. If Kwaku had a disaster plan in place, were the procedures the best ones?

DISPLAYS EVERYWHERE

How do I do it? wondered Alan, as he looked at his list of activities for the month. It was November, and the number of items seemed absolutely overwhelming. New to the Abraham Moses Middle School and new to the profession as a recent graduate from the Library Educational Media Program at the state college, Alan Den Uyl experienced a moment of panic.

Full of enthusiasm and ideas, Alan had stressed the concept of colorful displays that would highlight the library media center and show its connection with the curriculum and current events. In fact, that philosophy, plus his knowledge of computer graphics, had been a prime factor in his selection by the Board of Education for the position of library media specialist. Alan had presented the school administration and the board with a year-long plan for displays and bulletin boards that would be located in five different areas in the school. The proposal had been complete with text, a rationale, and impressive computer-generated graphics.

Now, it appeared that Alan had planned way beyond his means and abilities to adhere to the pace he had set for himself. He had devised a schedule for the construction of the displays and had considered involving students and parent volunteers in the project. He would be the facilitator, supply the ideas, locate materials, and print out the graphics, and the helpers would find the background materials and actually put the displays together.

Shortly after his first meeting with the students and volunteers, Alan set out to collect materials, book covers, and other realia for the displays, which would be located in four display cases and one exhibit bookcase with two locking glass display areas. He quickly discovered that the school library media center had little in the way of display materials and objects. He asked the art teacher if there were any colored paper sheets that he could have and, upon receiving a negative response, went after school to the local art store to purchase the necessary paper supplies with his own money.

The next day he began to look for books to place in the displays, but as he removed them from the shelves, he realized that he was decimating several areas of subjects and finding little to use on other topics. This appeared to be a problem. Then he thought of a possible solution. Why not copy the covers and place them in the display with notes about their locations on the shelves? And better yet, he could scan the covers on the computer and then print them out on his color copier at home. This seemed to be a feasible project.

The first night, Alan took about twenty books home and spent the entire evening scanning, editing, and printing out color computer prints of ten of the titles. It was not as easy as it first seemed! And then there was the problem of a lack of suitable materials on a particular subject. Alan thought he might be able to find titles on a related subject, and then he thought of searching for information on the Internet.

He had access at home, and on the third night, he began to search through the various sites and download graphics and text on selected subjects. It was interesting and fun, but very time-consuming and costly, as he printed out many pages before deciding which ones would be appropriate for the displays.

Then Alan realized that he needed some realia and put out a call to the teachers in the school, requesting selected objects that they might wish to loan to him for the exhibits. He received some answers, but they were all in the negative, since the teachers were using the objects in conjunction with their lessons. So, off to the store he went to purchase some statues and other materials. It was a costly venture.

The next step was to involve the volunteers, and Alan ran into problems with that, too. The parents, in particular, had their own ideas as to the construction of the displays, which were often at variance with Alan's plans. Multiple displays became fraught with difficulties and expense, and Alan began having doubts about the program. By this time, it was the end of October and the occasion to plan for November. Alan now considered his options . . .

Questions

1. Was Alan's plan reasonable? How many display areas can be covered with relative ease?
2. Should Alan have purchased materials from his own pocket?
3. How should Alan have handled the volunteer problems?
4. What should Alan do next?

VANDALISM HERE, THERE, AND EVERYWHERE

Fred Nyuaboga had read of acts of vandalism that occurred in schools. In fact, just last week the newspapers were filled with the story of a seventh-grader who had spray-painted the desks in the history classroom. There was talk in the teachers' room about a gang of youths that had damaged various facilities on the playground. And prior to that conversation was one about vandalism perpetrated in the library media center in another district school.

Fred had not thought much about that other library media center, since little interaction occurred between schools in the district. He reasoned that Riley School was in a different neighborhood where activities were more subdued, and the personal interactions between students and staff were much more cordial.

And now, all of a sudden, vandalism was an issue in Fred's own library media center! He came in early Monday morning as usual, carrying his briefcase full of papers and ideas for new programs, along with his cup of coffee. He reached the library media center, started to unlock the door, which was kept bolted to protect the computers, and realized that the door was already unbolted. He pushed it open and gazed with horror at the sight before him. The room was in disarray, with tables and chairs turned upside down. The walls, carpet, and books had been sprayed with some sort of foam, and the computers had been smashed. It was a sight almost too horrible for belief.

Fred picked his way through the debris to his office, with the thought of calling the principal to report the vandalism. To his dismay, the phone had been ripped off the desk and did not work. He put his briefcase and coffee on the only clean space he could find and retreated from the room. On his way to the office he encountered the custodian and blurted out his story, asking if Giorgio had noticed anyone in the building. Giorgio was indignant and accused Fred of blaming him for the damage. Fred denied that claim, and they proceeded together to the principal's office.

Alexis Jimenez, the school secretary, immediately called the police after hearing Fred's story. She asked Fred, who was rather distraught at this point, to sit in the principal's office until the police arrived. Sirens soon sounded in the distance, coming closer and closer until they were silenced right in front of the school. Officer Carlos Zavala entered the school and was ushered to the office through lines of students waiting for the school doors to open. He greeted Fred and asked the librarian to accompany him to the library media center.

Fred complied, and they walked down the hall as the officer asked questions about Fred's work, background, and personal life.

When they reached the library media center, Fred warned the officer about the condition of the floor and urged caution in walking through the glass and foam. Officer Zavala looked around the facility and whistled in exclamation at the extent of the damage. "Quite a mess," the officer commented, before asking Fred whether he had touched or moved anything in the room? Fred replied in the negative, and the officer remarked that was good and warned him not to touch anything until given permission. The policeman then asked Fred to return to the office to borrow paper, a marker, and the extra key for the library media center. He wanted Fred to hang a "Closed" sign on the door, without touching the lock, and lock the door from the inside, again without touching anything. Officer Zavala then used his cellular phone to call headquarters to request that dusting powder, a chemical sample kit, and cameras be brought to the school. He also requested that Fred stand by to identify items as they were photographed.

The second officer arrived, and they began the tedious work of dusting for fingerprints and taking pictures. Fred helped as much as he could, considering how upset he was about the condition of "his" library media center. He considered it almost a personal affront that the resources had been so horribly misused.

Later that day the police completed their investigation of the crime scene, promising to report the test results as soon as they were finalized. Then the clean-up began. The foam turned out to be a type of insulating foam, and it stuck onto the sprayed surfaces like glue. It was impossible to remove, and many items in the room had to be removed and destroyed.

By Thursday a semblance of order was restored to the library media center, and Fred reopened the room on a very limited schedule. Then came the reporter for the school newspaper, asking to interview Fred about what had happened. Fred described the scene and his discomfort. The student wrote the article, which appeared in the weekly paper. Fred was quoted at length, and the article ended with an appeal for the perpetrator to come forth and confess.

On Monday morning a note in Fred's mailbox directed him to report to the principal's office at 8:30. Fred walked in at the appointed time and was greeted by the principal holding the newspaper in his hand. Fred was dumbfounded by the principal's accusation that he had gone beyond the bounds of his rights in talking to the paper. The request for an interview should have gone through the proper channels, and Fred should have cleared it with the principal first. And certainly, Fred should not have discussed it with the press before the police report was made public!

Questions

1. What should Fred do next? Was the principal correct about the proper procedure for interviews?
2. Did Fred act in the best way after he discovered the vandalism?
3. Was talking to Giorgio the proper thing to do?
4. Should the secretary have called the police or the principal, assuming that the principal was in the building at the time?

MICEY, MICEY!

It all began when two of Evern Dock's students, who had been sitting quietly in the back of the school library media center doing their homework as part of an in-class detention, started looking around the room and cocking their ears. Then they began to giggle. When Evern asked them what was so funny, the girls replied that sounds of scratching were coming from the closet behind them and they supposed that he had a student locked up in there.

Evern was indignant and he quickly walked to the closet and opened the door. There was nothing in sight, and he admonished the girls for their silliness. Thus ended episode clue number one!

The next day clue number two surfaced. One of the boys in Evern's second-period class brought two books to the desk and opened them to the back, preparatory to checking them out. Directly inside the cover were some very ragged edges and little bits of paper, and yes, those telltale little brown nuggets. The student and Evern looked at each other and both had the same reaction at the same time. Signs of mice! Evern and the student walked over to the shelf where the books had been and saw more evidence. In fact, as they removed the rest of the books from the shelf, it was obvious that the mice had had a field day with all the volumes. They seemed to prefer the softer paper of the paperbacks, but they had tasted all of the books. Evern asked the student to keep this matter to himself and said that the problem would be promptly attended to. Then teacher and student went back to the desk to check out the original books, with a note inside ordering their repair upon return to the library media center.

Once the school library media center was empty of students and teachers, Evern put in a call to the custodial staff. Daisy was the first to respond, and she nearly fainted when she saw the evidence on the book shelves. Evern called for reinforcements, and when Rezwab arrived, he shoed Daisy away and the two men got busy, following clues to locate the pathway and the nest of the rodents. It was not an easy job, and the men ended up walking all around the media center, tracing a trail that on first look appeared to be merely dirt on the carpeting. Once they realized that the "dirt" was mouse droppings, they were horrified. The mice had apparently nibbled in various locations all around the center, and no one had ever noticed. It was amazing how insidious those little rodents were!

After a brief conference, they decided that an all-out attack was needed. Daisy by now had recovered, and she joined in the hunt. Every trail seemed to lead to a dead end—that is, except for one that led to the far corner where the cabinet containing the paper supplies was located. Rezwab carefully opened the cabinet and found what appeared to be the remains of a recently vacated nest. The mice were clever and seemed to know that they were the center of the great mouse chase.

The final bell of the day rang, and the human participants decided to call off the hunt until the next day. Rezwab announced that he was planning to stop at the hardware store on the way home and use the school's petty-cash funds to purchase some safe mouse traps. The salesperson recommended cheese as the bait, and Rezwab stopped at the supermarket to purchase the strongest-smelling cheese in the case. This accomplished, he headed home, taking care to leave the mouse traps in his car and to place the cheese in the refrigerator.

On day three Rezwab brought the traps and the cheese to school and set them up in the cabinets and the closets, places where students were unlikely to look and cause a major uproar. The day seemed extra long, and Evern resisted the temptation to open the doors and peek inside to see if any mice had been captured. Three thirty finally arrived, and after the school library media center was empty of students and faculty, Evern approached the cabinet and was delighted to hear muted sounds of little feet moving around on the shelves. He turned the handle and heard the sudden rush of feet scampering away. After the door was open, he could see the trap on the shelf, with more than half of the cheese removed, but no mice inside. Somehow they had managed to get out of the humane trap. Then Evern realized that he and Rezwab had not set up the trap properly and that the mice were able to slither through the openings and slither back out again. Evern readjusted the trap mechanism and replaced the cheese that had been eaten. He hoped that the mice were not satiated from their feast and would return and be trapped during the night.

Day four was the big day of the mouse chase. Evern found four mice inside the cabinet trap and three in the closet trap. What was he to do next? He called for Rezwab, who removed the traps and their inhabitants in a covered cart. Both men breathed a sigh of relief that the chase was over and that the mice had never once made an appearance to frighten students or faculty. The rodents had worked undercover, which made their detection more difficult and probably prolonged the time when they could damage the media center. But at least it was over!

Questions

1. How could the men be sure the mouse chase/invasion was over?
2. Up to this point, no mention was made of tracking down the entry point for the mice and/or their current nest. What should Evern do next?

3. Neither was mention made of contacting and involving the school administrators in the problem. Should this have been done? Perhaps the mice invasion was taking place in other locations as well.
4. What should Evern do with the books that had sections eaten away by the mice?

• *3* •

Personal

CRUSHES

Richard Perez was both puzzled and annoyed. He had found cute little love notes at the end of the stacks, attached to the book ends, on the blotter on his desk, and stuck to the corners of the circulation computer. They were short little bits of doggerel, all proclaiming undying love or making complimentary comments on his curly hair, his glasses, or his suits. None of the notes used his name as a point of address. They just seemed to appear out of nowhere at different times of the day.

Richard's reaction of annoyance was due in part to the idea that "his" school library media center was the location for either a prank or a lovesick student who was trying to contact another student. Richard had always viewed "his" media center as a place for research and class-related instruction. It was certainly not designed as a counseling center or as a romantic meeting place where two students could exchange verses.

His puzzlement was due to a desire to find out to whom and by whom the notes were contrived. Richard spot-checked the location of the notes periodically during the day and never noticed anyone near them. He also did not notice any particular student or students who seemed to be in the media center at the time of the notes' placement.

Richard felt challenged and decided to ask the computer teacher, Melissa Graham, for advice on how to handle the situation. Melissa looked at the notes collected by Richard and began to laugh. She quickly suppressed her mirth and asked Richard with great seriousness if he realized that the notes were directed at him—that he was the target of someone's affection. After looking at the notes again, Richard rather shamefacedly admitted that Melissa was probably right and he hadn't even considered that possibility prior to that time. After a few shared laughs, Melissa and Richard decided that they had better try to identify the lovelorn person. The notes had been typed on a computer and cute little graphics had been hand-drawn and colored around the text. The hearts and XXs appeared to be the work of a girl, most likely a student.

The conclusion seemed to narrow down the search a bit, and Melissa and Richard decided to plan a scientific, efficient method of detection. Richard was to keep careful watch on the students as they walked around the school library media center and to note the names of all the girl students who entered the facility.

Melissa was dispatched to check the schedules of girls in art and writing classes to see if any overlap of visits to the library media center occurred during the day. Her quest revealed three students who had schedules that allowed them to visit the library, either as part of a class or for independent study. She informed Richard of the three names and suggested that he watch them particularly carefully.

Richard agreed to do this and spent the next two days observing the girls whenever they entered the library media center. It was funny; he had never particularly noticed them before, but now he was aware of their mannerisms. The girls entered the room at different times, so Richard was able to watch each one rather closely. Then, all of a sudden, Richard realized that student number two, Theresa, was observing him as he watched her. His eyes were wary, hers were sparkling and dreamy at the same time. Their eyes connected and hers sent him a message of love. Richard knew then who the note writer was. Now, what to do next? Was Theresa acting alone? Did she manage to contrive frequent excuses to visit the center and place all the notes herself? Or did she have accomplices who placed the notes around the room for her when she was in class? Was this an invasion of privacy? Or did Theresa just have a crush on him? Was this serious and a violation of school policy? All those thoughts rushed through Richard's mind as he pondered what to do about the situation.

Questions

1. What should Richard do?
2. Were those valid questions that Richard asked himself?
3. Could a crush by a student on a school library media specialist be dangerous?
4. Could it have been just a prank? Or was it possible that Theresa really did place Richard among her heroes?
5. Was this a matter for the school authorities, or should Richard try to handle it himself?

THERE ALL THE TIME

Here he comes again, Laura sighed to herself. This was the third time in the past half hour that Wartyna Allison had approached her with a question. A seventh-grader, Wartyna seemed to have an insatiable curiosity about everything. He was interested in all aspects of the school library media center and spent every study period there, as well as the regular class sessions when the students learned about the more sophisticated research tools housed in the center.

To Laura, it was almost an illusion of constant attendance. And to make matters worse, it seemed not only that he was always there but that he constantly asked questions and interrupted her conversations with other students. When this happened, she gently chastised Wartyna and he apologized to the other people. Laura had hoped that this situation would eventually resolve itself as Wartyna gained more social skills. Wartyna was new to the school the past September, and at first the attention he paid to Laura and her media center had been rather flattering. But her feelings soon turned to annoyance, as Wartyna unwittingly continued to pester her.

As Wartyna opened his mouth to ask yet another question, it took all of her self-control for Laura to smile and resist the urge to make a negative comment. She did not want to insult him or discourage his quest for knowledge but found it very difficult to restrain herself. Wartyna's question was very simple and one he most likely could have answered himself. Laura responded with a rather curt reply, and Wartyna looked surprised. He didn't say anything other than to thank her for her answer and then returned to his seat. He spent the rest of the period glancing over at Laura with a rather puzzled and reproachful expression.

As the students left the school library media center, Laura made a point of saying good-bye to Wartyna. His good-bye was stilted and uttered in a low voice. Laura felt terrible. What should she have done? A student who monopolizes the school library media specialist's time can be very disruptive and take away the attention needed by other students. As she thought back upon the situation, Laura realized that the other students had begun to ask questions of each other rather than approach her for help. They had apparently been discouraged by Wartyna's attention to her.

At this point, Laura decided to talk to the school's guidance counselor. She stopped by his office during her planning period, while a parent volunteer covered the school library media center. Charles Aylin was happy to see her and invited her to have a seat so they could discuss an issue that had been brought to his attention. When Laura mentioned the name of Wartyna Allison, she grimaced and turned all her attention to Charles. He began by telling her that Wartyna had visited him the past afternoon and was rather disturbed. Wartyna was concerned that he had offended Laura and had asked Charles what he could do to correct the situation. Charles had been working with Wartyna as a student new to the school, and one who came from a very difficult home life. Wartyna often spoke to Charles of Laura as a caring and special person who gave him some of the attention he craved and didn't get in his other classes or at home. Her abrupt answer in class had upset him and he perceived it as a lack of attention. Laura agreed that could have been possible, and she also felt that something needed to be done.

Charles and Laura decided that the time had come to have a meeting with Wartyna. Charles contacted the student's homeroom teacher and asked to have Wartyna come to his office the next day, right after the morning announcements and before the first period. At that time Laura had a parent aide available to cover the media center, so she would be free to meet with Charles and Wartyna.

In the meeting Charles took the lead, stressing that Laura and everyone else in the school was anxious to help Wartyna, but that he needed to develop certain social skills to aid in the process. Wartyna asked about those skills, and Laura and Charles gently told him about consideration for others and the need to ask constructive questions, rather than simple or purely rhetorical ones. Wartyna listened with rapt attention and agreed with all the points. He answered that he would try hard to pay attention to the suggestions and be more cooperative in his interactions with others. He apologized to Laura and promised to be very careful in the library media center. The meeting ended and everyone seemed to be pleased.

Questions

1. Should Laura have tolerated the situation this long before doing something about it?
2. Should she have done more to encourage Wartyna to answer his questions on his own?
3. Should Laura have looked beyond Wartyna's questions and behavior for symptoms or causes, or is that the responsibility of the guidance counselor? Is it important for teachers and school library media specialists who are trained as teachers to understand student psychology?
4. Did Charles and Laura use the proper technique in working with Wartyna? What might have happened if Wartyna refused to acknowledge his problems and became defensive during the conference? What should Charles and Laura have done then?

HERE THEY COME!

"Oh, no, it can't be!" was the reaction of Cindy MacDonald as she saw the group of students walking through the doors of the school library media center. She had heard parts of a conversation in the staff room, while having lunch the day before. Snatches of details had come through the general lunchtime buzz, about three boys and four girls who had formed a gang that was causing trouble in the school.

Cindy recognized one student's name and could hardly believe her ears. Brian Soto had been one of her student aides and was a quiet, efficient worker. The name of a second student sounded familiar, but Cindy was not as sure of it as she was of Brian's. Unfortunately, the teacher who made the remark left the room before Cindy could collect her wits and make further inquiries. The two teachers with whom she had lunched didn't recognize any of the students mentioned, so Cindy was left feeling rather upset.

Cindy had an important meeting to attend after school so had no opportunity to ask any further questions about the gang that day. She arrived home somewhat late in the evening and didn't feel right about calling any of her colleagues at that hour. She could only wait and see what would happen.

And now was the time. Coming through the doors and detection gate were the four students, including Brian, who looked rather different than Cindy remembered him. Cindy decided not to say anything to Brian or any of the other students and just wait to see what happened. She continued her work on a project about inventors with a group of students at the table.

Then Cindy felt a sudden chill. Out of the corner of her eye she saw the gang walk over to the nonfiction stacks and begin to rearrange some books on each shelf. Next, they approached the bank of computers and removed the CDs from each computer that was not in use. The computers were not networked, and Cindy had separate programs on each station. A sign over each CD slot warned users not to touch, but the gang members completely ignored them. They then walked over to the work area that was supposed to be out of bounds to non–school library media center personnel and proceeded to pull out and empty the drawers from the old shelflist and pull old issues of periodicals off the shelves.

At this point Cindy decided that enough was enough. So far, few other students using the media center had noticed what the gang was doing, and there was no commotion. The gang members were not noisy, they were just destructive. Cindy left the inventor group working away and walked over to the work room. She confronted the gang members, speaking primarily to Brian, and asked them what they were doing. One student seemed to be the spokesperson, and he replied that they just felt like messing up the school library media center. Cindy again tried to speak to Brian, but the spokesperson said that Brian was just following orders and that Cindy had no hold over him.

Then the gang members, including Brian, began to chant lines such as "No more teachers, no more librarians, no more books" while they walked around Cindy. She felt threatened and shouted that she was going to call the principal. At this, all the other students looked around to see what the commotion was about and began whispering among themselves. Cindy spotted a girl sitting at one of the tables and recognized her as a student aide who helped in the media center. Cindy, surrounded by the chanting and circling gang members, motioned to the student to go to the phone and call for help. Melody grasped the seriousness of the situation and quickly called the office for help on the intercom. The response from the office was quick. The principal and the vice principal came running down the hall and into the school library media center.

There was no security guard in this suburban high school, but one of the custodians was a big burly man who rushed into the media center from another direction. All three men converged on the work room, but the principal stopped for a minute to ask all the other students to leave the center. Seeing the force that was about to descend upon them, the gang members quickly stopped chanting and broke up their circle around Cindy, who then moved away from them. The principal asked for an accounting of what had happened, and Cindy described the various acts of destruction that the gang had committed. The students stood there with smirks on their faces as the damages were recorded by the vice principal. Then the students were marched out of the media center and to the office.

Cindy was shaken and sat down to collect her wits. The principal had requested that she report to the office after the last class period of the day and close the media center at that time. She could put a note on the door, indicating that an emergency had arisen and that the center would reopen the next day. Cindy was not to rearrange any of the misplaced materials until she had made a complete inventory of the damage.

Then Cindy remembered the students who had been asked to leave the media center. Were they still in the hallway or had they dispersed? She wanted to thank Melody for her help and to reassure the students that the ordeal was over and that the damage could be repaired. But, alas, there was no one in sight.

Questions

1. Did Cindy follow the best method for handling the situation?
2. Should she have acted sooner?
3. Would it have been better for her to have taken some time before the after-school meeting to find out more about the gang from the school administration or fellow teachers?
4. What do you think should happen to the gang members? If the damage they caused could be relatively easily replaced and rearranged, was there a need for punitive measures?

STORIES, STORIES, STORIES

Ikira Dries, the new school library media specialist in the Rhodes School, walked into the teacher's room to eat lunch. The buzz of conversation that could be heard almost out in the hall ceased instantly, and the teachers all looked down at their places. Ikira said hello and received a quiet murmur of response, but nothing else. She got a cup of coffee from the machine and then sat down at her usual table, opened her lunch bag, and started to eat her sandwich. The only sound to be heard was of people munching on apples and carrots.

Then, suddenly, there was a rustle of lunch bags being crumpled up and thrown in the garbage can and footsteps of teachers leaving the room. There were no "good-byes," just quick departures. Ikira was puzzled and began to look at her plan book, which she had carried into the room with her. She heard the sound of a door opening, and Ana Fuentes walked into the room. When she spotted Ikira, she quickly turned around and walked back out again. It was very strange!

After lunch, Ikira decided that she needed to find out what was happening. She had three classes to teach that afternoon, but once they were completed she had some free time in her schedule. She asked Ida, the library aide, to cover the school library media center and she went down the hall to Ana's classroom. Ana was just finishing a lesson, and Ikira motioned to her that she had something to discuss. Ana nodded and indicated that she would be free in a few minutes. Ikira waited for her, and once Ana had dismissed her students for the day, she beckoned for Ikira to join her in the back of the classroom. They sat on adjacent seats and commenced a long discussion.

Ana apologized for her actions in the teachers' room when she walked out on Ikira. She explained that she had been afraid that someone would see her talking to Ikira, and she did not want to make a bad situation worse. When Ikira asked Ana what she meant by a bad situation, Ana replied that she felt caught in the middle of a vicious rumor mill. She explained as gently as she could that Ikira was the victim of stories that were being spread by a teacher in the school who was a qualified school library media specialist and had applied for Ikira's job.

When Ikira was hired for the position, the teacher, Angelyna Easterling, was very upset because she thought that she deserved the job. Even though some of Angelyna's friends told her that she should apply for another library media position in another district school, Angelyna refused to consider their suggestions. Before this, she had been very happy in Rhodes School and had counted on receiving the media specialist position when the former librarian retired. She had not even considered that any question would arise over her becoming the next media specialist. The principal liked her and thought she had some good ideas about the school library media center. The vice principal was not quite as enthusiastic as the principal, but he had told Angelyna that he considered her a viable candidate for the position.

It came as quite a shock when the principal announced to the teachers that the administration was offering the position to Ikira, an "outside" candidate who had experience as a library media specialist but did not know Rhodes School or the students. Angelyna had argued that Ikira would need quite a bit of orientation and acclimation to the school and its library media center and that she, Angelyna, came already prepared and oriented. Her statements were to no avail, and Ikira was hired for the position.

Angelyna bided her time for the month of September. When Ikira appeared to be making friends and establishing a rapport with the students, it was obvious that she was not about to leave, either through disciplinary action from the administration or voluntarily. Angelyna decided that the time had come to force the issue—but by stealth, not challenge.

That was when the rumors began to circulate around the school. Very subtly, Angelyna made little innuendoes to fellow teachers about Ikira, an attractive and vivacious woman, and her extracurricular activities and the way in which she had achieved the position. A comment here, a comment there, and soon the rumors became vicious.

Ana was a good friend of Ikira's, and she was upset to hear the stories. She resolved to let Ikira know about them, but she was afraid to involve herself in the situation. So she waited until she could speak privately to Ikira. She wasn't sure what Ikira would do, but at least Ikira would know what was happening.

Questions

1. What should Ikira do? The situation appears to be intolerable and if Ikira wants to keep her job, she will need to do something.
2. Should Ana openly help her friend in whatever action she decides to undertake?
3. Should the principal and vice principal be involved in this?
4. Should Ikira approach the other teachers and ask to tell her side of the story? Or should she simply ignore the situation and hope that Angelyna will give up?

SMOKING IN THE BOYS' ROOM

Ricardo Ramirez has been a social studies teacher in the middle school at Union Grove Township for the last three years. He is singularly uninspiring and has a great deal of difficulty with classroom management. State requirements for certification require the completion of a master's degree in a subject field for full certification. This graduate degree must be completed within four years of initial certification. The requirement seems tailor-made for Ricardo. He decides to complete this requirement by getting a master's degree in Library and Information Sciences.

Because of the existing bargaining unit agreement, Ricardo can actually complete his degree requirements in the MLS Program and then transfer to an existing vacancy in a school library media center. He begins his program of study and, by taking two courses a semester and three in the summer, is able to leave his middle school social studies classroom in record time. Upon completion of his MLS and new certificate, he transfers to a large middle school as the second school library media specialist.

Ricardo works with Beth Alonzo, an experienced school library media specialist. Beth is considered the technology guru for the Union Grove District, and as a result, Chartwell Middle School houses an impressive array of state-of-the-art technology. Ricardo tells Beth that he is willing to learn, and the two of them collaborate on many projects. Beth is pleased to have Ricardo to work with, although she notices that he often lags in energy in the afternoon. He seems really enthusiastic in the mornings and immediately after lunch, but as the afternoon progresses, Ricardo seems to become short-tempered and sluggish. He leaves promptly at 3:30 P.M., citing child-care responsibilities.

Nance Milo is the principal at Chartwell, and she and Beth are friendly, both during and after the workday. One afternoon, Beth confides to Nance that she thinks Ricardo may be diabetic. She says he often seems lethargic and sometimes has a candy bar, which seems to revive him. Nance tells Beth she will have the school nurse stop by for an informal chat.

At the end of the next week, the Union Grove School District has its required Teacher Training Day. This full day of training offers an opportunity for many of the school library media specialists to visit one another's library media centers. Beth and Ricardo host all of the other middle school library media specialists for the morning. They are then free to work together in the afternoon on their library media center's Web page. Ricardo excuses himself about 2:30 P.M. and goes to the lavatory. He returns about five minutes later. He makes a comment to Beth about the hollowness of the halls without students and teachers in attendance.

Just at this time, Nance comes into the library media center. She motions Beth to come with her. They head down the hall in the direction of the men's room. Nance opens the door and tells Beth to step in. Beth immediately recognizes the smell—marijuana. Nance tells Beth that Ricardo is the only man on the second floor at this time—and in fact, for the last hour since Louis, the custodian, went to lunch. Nance tells Beth that she thinks Ricardo is smoking pot on the job and that in fact he is probably smoking regularly on the job, hence his bouts of sluggishness. Beth is shocked but tells Nance she will keep her eyes and ears alert to this potentially dangerous situation.

Questions

1. Was Beth correct in confiding her suspicions about Ricardo's diabetes to Nance?
2. What should Nance, as the principal, have done upon hearing about Ricardo's potential health problem?
3. Is Nance jumping to an inaccurate conclusion regarding Ricardo's drug use?
4. Is Nance leaving herself and Union Grove School District open to a lawsuit?
5. What should Beth do in terms of observing Ricardo's behavior?
6. What should be done immediately upon smelling marijuana?

IS THIS DISCRIMINATION?

Harmon Scott is the sixth-grade language arts teacher at the Lake Washington Middle School. He is a young teacher and eager to make his mark with his students. He teaches to the high standards promoted through the National Center for Education and the Economy (NCEE) and wants his students not only to meet but also to exceed those standards. He requires a written book report every other week from a list that he and the library media specialist have jointly compiled. He has quiet reading time as part of his daily class work and models the behavior that he wants his students to follow. As part of his emphasis on teaching to standards, Harmon requires that his students keep a journal about their reading. This journal is a continuous log not only of summaries of what the students have read but of responses to that writing. Harmon has numerous prompts that the students may select to respond to. This writing is in addition to his required bimonthly book reports.

Tiqua Johnson, like Harmon Scott, is a dedicated professional. Tiqua is the library media specialist at Lake Washington. As is Harmon, she is young and eager to make her mark with her students. She has worked at Lake Washington for about five years—two more than Harmon. Tiqua is familiar with teaching to high standards and has completed Course One of the NCEE Program.

Although Tiqua and Harmon have much in common, their approaches are very different. Harmon is a methodical worker. He plans his program over the summer, sketching out objectives and goals. He corresponds with each student and his or her family prior to the start of the school year. He lays out for them what he hopes to accomplish during the year.

Each quarter, he revises his plan. He is not lock-stepped into his plan, but he feels that middle school students need structure. He offers them a structured program in language arts that ensures success for a large number of students. On the statewide writing assessment, Harmon's pass ratio is among the highest.

Sometimes, however, Harmon is seen by his peers and the parents of his students as too structured. He has his rubrics and the standards posted in his classroom. He consistently refers his students to them. Sometimes the students miss the point, but instead of reteaching, Harmon moves forward. He feels that those who fail to meet or understand that particular standard or to follow a certain rubric will catch up or catch on as time progresses. As a result of this approach, there is often an undercurrent of animosity and anger in his classroom by children who are not successful. Harmon ignores this and simply pushes onward.

Several times parents have accused him of being too structured and of ignoring their child. Many times these complaints come from the parents of children of color. Tiqua works closely with Harmon—identifying appropriate materials for his assignments, helping students to select materials of interest and formulate their journal responses based upon research about the author or genre. Harmon has several times accused her in a friendly but firm manner of providing too much assistance to the students. He feels that she often spoon-feeds his students. Tiqua is confident of her work and her abilities, and although she keeps her personal feelings about Harmon to herself, she does feel that he is just too structured and demanding for middle-grade students. She respects him for being a hard worker but, as a woman of color, sometimes feels that he is too hard on minority children. Although Tiqua has never spoken with Harmon about her feelings, she does notice that a large percentage of his minority children do not achieve the standard on the state testing. She notices that there appears to be a predictable equity gap. Furthermore, she notices but does not comment on what appears to her to be a lack of diversified teaching strategies. He has his routine and does not deviate.

This year, Harmon appears to be in trouble. He has had several incidents in the classroom where student behavior was so out-of-hand that the administration had to be summoned. Harmon looks haggard and at lunch bad-mouths a number of his students. He actually has spoken about transferring to another school, perhaps even a private school where the "students really want to learn." The final straw for Harmon has been the accusation that his behavior is racially biased. During a recent confrontation with a student, Harmon told the child that his "true colors" were showing. The child, who is African-American, reported the comment to his mother. The mother has filed a complaint with the school and with the Office of Equity for the district. Tiqua feels caught in the middle, as she knows the mother socially from her church. She knows that the child often has experienced frustration in his language arts class but is indeed no angel.

Questions

1. Should Tiqua share her feelings about Harmon with anyone?
2. If you feel that she should, with whom? The principal? The parent? The district director of equity?
3. What did Harmon mean by this phrase? Is it racist or just an expression that is out-of-date but nonetheless used by a language arts professional?
4. Should Harmon have modified his teaching strategies to allow for diverse learning styles?
5. Can you argue with his successful pass ratio?
6. How can you determine the validity of Tiqua's feelings about an equity gap in the statewide testing results from Harmon's students?

• *4* •

Personnel

AFTER HOURS AND THE UNION

It was an exciting day for Diana Bakarich, the school library media specialist at Pearl River School. Her classes had been well received by the students, her book talk was evaluated by the principal and he declared that it was exciting and compelling for him, the teacher, and the students. And as if that was not enough, she received a note in her mailbox that her special order of books had arrived and was ready to be picked up!

Diana had submitted a grant for a collection of multicultural books to be used by the increasing number of students from other cultures who were entering the school system. The grant had been awarded and Diana received five boxes of reference books, student resources, and teacher aids to be added to her collection. The school newspaper had featured an article about the grant when Diana learned that she was the recipient and had subsequently published snippets of reminders about the subject. This was a great opportunity for the school, and everyone seemed to be very happy about it.

The boxes were delivered by the custodian to the school library media center, and Diana began to open the first one. She removed the packing slip and took the first volume out of the box. As she was about to place it on the book truck next to the table, she noticed that the book had no spine label. She opened the book to the back and saw no date due slip. Diana then looked for a copy of the requisition form in the box. When she didn't see it in that box, she opened another carton, hoping that the form would be in that one. In the last box Diana found the copy she had been seeking. She quickly scanned it, saw the list of titles and the price for each volume, and then looked for any other details. She was searching for a charge for preprocessing the volumes and for tape-loading of the titles into the library media center's automated system. There was no evidence of any extra levies.

Diana then pulled out her copy of the grant application and was horrified to note that the item for the preprocessing and tape-loading of MARC records was not checked. How could this have happened? Diana had looked over the form numerous times before submitting it and had even had the vice principal double-check it. Neither of them had noticed the omission. With a sigh, Diana walked down to the vice principal's office to share the news.

John Flannery, the vice principal, was as dismayed as she and remarked that it looked as if the new book project would be delayed even longer than they had expected. He suggested that Diana work out a method for processing the materials and entering the titles into the database as soon as possible. He left Diana to come up with ideas on how to do this and departed for a meeting. Diana went back to the school library media center and began to think of ways to cope with the situation. Five boxes of books were quite a lot and, at that point, seemed overwhelming. Diana decided to approach the problem methodically, opened all the boxes, and placed the books on book trucks. She separated them into categories of reference, fiction, non-fiction, biography, and teacher aids. She then subdivided them into Dewey numbers in each category and arranged the fiction by author. She figured that would help with linking the titles and providing Dewey numbers as needed.

Once that was done, Diana began to think about the supplies she would need for the project. She needed book plates, date due slips, spine labels, and barcode labels. She looked through the supplies in the back room and found that she had just about enough to use for the new books. She had kept a supply of processing items for use when she needed to catalog gift items, and her backlog could be used for the new multicultural books. That was a relief!

Next came the thought about how and when to work on the project. Diana had a free period every day, and there were parent volunteers who helped out in the library media center. The parents shelved materials and assisted with shelf arrangement, circulation, and storytelling. They had very little time for anything else. Diana's one free period per day would not allow for much to be accomplished on this big project. Diana felt as if she needed at least forty-eight hours in every day.

Then, suddenly, it came to her. She could stay after school two hours every day to catalog and process the books. She would use a batch process whereby she would classify all the volumes and then process each grouping with the appropriate book plates, date due slips, and spine labels. Finally, she would enter each title into the database by category, because once the book and item record had been keyed into the system it would indicate that the volume was available for use on the shelf. Diana always linked the records just before she placed the new books on the shelves, and this pleased the library media center users because they could be assured of the location of the title.

This would be an efficient use of her time and would help to make the multicultural collection available for research and reading as soon as possible. Diana was pleased with her idea and stayed in the school library media center after the students, parents, and other teachers had left each afternoon. When she went to her mailbox on the fourth day, she found a note addressed to her as the "overtime lady." The note had been written by the building union representative, and it stated in no uncertain terms that Diana was violating the union contract by staying after hours. Diana was thunderstruck and went straight to the vice principal's office.

Questions

1. What should Diana do next?
2. Should she have cleared her plan of work with the vice principal? Could Diana could have solved her problem any other way?
3. Should the school have backed Diana with help since the administration had erred when it checked Diana's grant application?
4. Would it be feasible to ask for volunteers to help with the project during the school day? Could volunteers be taught to

classify by Dewey when there was no Cataloging in Publication information in the book, and/or could they be trained to use the cataloging information?
5. Would a possible solution be for the school to hire some library workers from a professional library agency to catalog, link, and process the titles? Would there be enough time for Diana to supervise their work?

I DARE YOU!

It happened again today! Zenia Torres was left alone with the class during period five. She was in the middle of teaching the children research skills, and Rogae Thomas, the sixth-grade teacher, just walked out of the school library media center. After Zenia completed the lesson and was lining the students up to leave the media center, Rogae appeared from down the hallway. He took over the direction of the class, acting as if absolutely nothing had happened.

Never mind that the school regulations mandated that the teacher remain with the class in the school library media center during lessons and free selection time. Never mind that the school administration had made it clear that the library period was not a substitute teaching time for the teacher or that the school library media specialist was not supposed to be a cover for the teacher. It seemed as if Rogae was determined to make his own rules.

The first occurrence of this behavior had evidenced itself several weeks earlier when Rogae had interrupted Zenia's lessons to announce that he needed to make an emergency phone call. Zenia had graciously covered the class herself, and Rogae had returned within a few minutes. The next time Rogae had wandered out of the room shortly before the end of the lesson and had returned as the period ended, apologizing to Zenia as an aside. He did the same thing the following week, discreetly uttering his apology as he led the class from the media center.

Zenia had mixed feelings about the situation. Rogae seemed to be violating the regulations, but he had apologized, implying that there was a good reason for his absence. Zenia was reluctant to say anything about the situation to her supervisor or to the school administration because Rogae appeared to be sorry for what he was doing. However, there was a danger that someone else would notice what was happening and begin either to question the breaking of the rules or to do the same thing.

Zenia decided to wait and see what would happen and not do anything about the situation for the moment. The students did not seem to mind if the teacher left the room, so why should she? Her lessons and library routines were successful, and Zenia had learned the names of all the students and was able to keep the peace on her own. Why create a problem if everything seemed to be going along with or without Rogae?

Then, on the fifth week Rogae Thomas left the media center as soon as he had delivered the class to Zenia. There was no eye contact to indicate that Rogae was on a mission, just a simple walk out the door. Zenia taught the class and watched as Rogae returned as the lesson ended. The "usual" apology was not offered and Rogae simply ordered the students to follow him down the hall. Zenia was disappointed that Rogae offered no gesture of thanks or explanation, and she began to reassess her approach to the situation.

It seemed as if a real problem was developing. Zenia suddenly realized that Rogae was in essence daring her to tell on him. She had been an innocent accomplice to his actions and to tell on him would be to admit that she had allowed him to use her as a cover for some time. It was an interesting dilemma, and Zenia was not sure which way to turn. As she thought about it, she also realized that there seemed to be little reinforcement of the lessons she had taught the students. One of the reasons for having the teacher in the media center during the library session was so that the teacher could know what the students had been taught and could build upon the skills during the week. It seemed as if Zenia was going almost back to "square one" every week when her lessons began.

So, in addition to breaking the rules, Rogae was shortchanging his students and making double work for Zenia. That was not fair to the students or to the media specialist.

Once Zenia put all the pieces together, she realized that something had to be done. She waited until the end of the day and, after making sure that the media center was empty, she walked to the office and asked to speak to the principal. The secretary said that he was out of the office at present but was due back shortly. Zenia said that she would wait and sat in the office anteroom.

Gerald Alexander, the principal, was surprised to see Zenia waiting for him. Zenia was usually to be found in the media center and, except for budget requests, had had little contact with him. When she told him of her problem, Gerald was shocked and dismayed.

Questions

1. What do you think the principal did about the situation?
2. Was Zenia correct in first speaking to the principal rather than to Rogae?
3. When do you think Zenia should have acted on this situation?
4. Is the lack of follow-up and reinforcement a valid reason for the policy of teacher attendance?
5. Can you think of any other reason(s) for the policy?

GO SIT IN THE CORNER!

It did not seem as if it mattered whether the day was sunny or overcast. It did not seem to matter whether the day was warm, hot, or cold. Desiree McDonald was the school library media specialist in the Hoffman School, and she was trying to figure out a rationale for the behavior of Justin Harris, a sixth-grader who always seemed to be in trouble. She was also trying to find a reason why Mr. Khan, the principal, had completely dismissed the situation. Perhaps Justin was just clumsy or hyperactive. Desiree had learned of students who are just filled with energy and caused trouble. Justin always seemed to be in the middle of whatever commotion was raised in the media center. Desiree did not want to single him out as a mischief maker, but that seemed to be exactly what he was.

She thought back to the day when Justin had walked—no, he almost ran—around the end of the book stacks and crashed into a book truck filled with books for reshelving. Justin did not seem to be in the least bit hurt or apologetic; he just left the truck and books on the floor and exited the media center. Desiree did not know whether she should be annoyed or concerned. She had asked a student assistant to help her, and together they picked up the books and placed them on the uprighted truck. There was no follow-up of that incident.

Then Desiree remembered the time when Justin picked a word fight with one of the students who was studying at his table. Desiree broke up the dispute and separated the students. Justin was the instigator of the argument, and Desiree threatened him with punishment if he did it again. Justin looked at Desiree with a smirk, and he mumbled something about people minding their own business. Desiree ignored the remark and went back to charging out books for other students.

And then another incident occurred that very day. Once again, Justin provoked a dispute with a girl who was looking for books. He had wanted to find a book in the same section of book shelves as the other student, and he just pushed her out of the way. In fact, he pushed her so hard that she fell onto the floor. Fortunately, the floor was carpeted, so the girl was not injured, at least not physically. She walked over to Miss McDonald and complained about Justin's behavior and her hurt feelings. Desiree immediately approached Justin and asked him what had happened. He refused to answer her, and that is when she told him to report to the principal's office. Enough was enough, and it was time for Justin's bad behavior to be stopped.

Desiree called down to the office to make sure that Justin had reported in. The secretary confirmed that he had and remarked that she had a feeling that the result of the principal/student interview would not be good. Desiree hung up the phone, wondering what the secretary had meant by that remark.

She turned around, and there was Justin walking through the door of the media center. When Desiree asked him what had happened, he replied that Mr. Khan had believed his story that the girl had been the precipitator of the incident and that Miss McDonald had punished the wrong person. He looked absolutely pleased with himself.

Desiree did not believe Justin's story, but she was alone with the class in the media center and no other adult was in the room. She did not want to leave the media center untended, so she decided to wait until after school hours to talk with Mr. Khan.

When 3:30 finally came, Desiree went down to the administrative office. Ruma Khan was just walking out the door, and Desiree stopped him and asked if she could talk with him for a few minutes. Ruma agreed, and they went into his office and sat at his table. Desiree told him her side of the story, not only of the incident that had occurred that day, but of those on previous days that she had ignored. Ruma's reply, when Desiree had completed her tale, was that she had not acted properly and had not taken the correct measures to correct Justin's behavior on her own, so he wouldn't do anything to help her. Desiree was absolutely dismayed at that pronouncement and immediately left Ruma Khan's office.

Questions

1. What should Desiree do next?
2. Was Ruma Khan's analysis of the situation correct? Did Desiree wait too long to do anything?
3. Should the union be involved in this situation?
4. Is it possible that there is a medical cause of Justin's behavior? Rather than arguing about punishment, should the school library media specialist and the principal be concerned about having Justin tested?
5. Where do Justin's parents fit into the equation?

WHERE IS LARRY?

Valerie stared at the walls above the book stacks in the school library media center. Quite a bit of white space existed above those six-foot-high shelves, and Valerie wanted very much to fill that space.

Her gaze went from the walls to the neatly stacked posters she had purchased. Valerie Valentin, the media specialist, had taken the pictures to a frame store and had had them carefully and tastefully framed for hanging. The illustrations were of characters from children's literature, and Valerie thought they would be a welcome addition to the media center. They would brighten up the room, and Valerie had ideas of using them as focal points for book talks and literature lessons.

It had seemed to be a great idea, a great concept in the planning, but in the final execution, it did not seem as if the idea would even come about. Valerie had filled out a work order to have the posters hung, and nothing happened. When Valerie encountered Larry Owens, the custodian, in the hallway and asked him when he planned to hang her pictures, Larry gave her a very strange answer. He stated that he did not plan to ever do it and, most certainly, would not hang pictures for a woman, especially for a Hispanic woman. Valerie was shocked at that response and retorted that she would do it herself or have a friend do it.

Larry laughed when he heard Valerie's reply. He informed her that she could not reach that high, even if she stood on the table. He would most certainly not give her his custodial ladder, and he doubted that she could manage to carry a ladder of her own into the school. Besides, the union had regulations against faculty members doing custodial work themselves. He said that he would report her to the union if she persisted in trying to hang the pictures herself.

Valerie then mentioned Larry's sexist remark and stated that she intended to do something about it. Larry responded with a laugh, remarking that there was nothing she could do about it.

Valerie thought to herself that Larry was mistaken on that point, and she walked away from him. She returned to the media center and sat at her desk to think things out.

Questions

1. What should Valerie do next?
2. What are the steps that should be followed in a sexist/racist situation?
3. Was Valerie's idea of decorating the school library media center valid?
4. Should Valerie check on the validity of Larry's statement that the union was opposed to teaching staff members doing their own decorating and maintenance work. Do you think Larry was referring to the union that represented the custodial staff or the union to which teachers and other staff members belonged?

THE LIBRARY MEDIA CENTER AS PUNISHMENT ROOM

Susan Dedham is the sixth-grade language arts teacher at the Lakeland Elementary School. The school is the largest in the district, with an enrollment of over 900 students. There are two full-time library media specialists, and both are flexibly scheduled. One full-time clerk has been with the two full-time library media specialists for the last five years. The three staff members work well together and strive to create a friendly but purposeful atmosphere in the library media center.

The physical plant at Lakeland Elementary is large enough to accommodate two classes in the library media center at the same time. There is a separate, carpeted storytelling area, an informal spot with recreational reading materials, magazines, and newspapers, as well as a more formal instructional area. Here, students are seated at tables and chairs with reference books, CD workstations, and Internet stations in close proximity. A large-screen television sits in a central area, which can be used for instructional purposes—staff members can demonstrate using search engines, using Power Point for instructional guidance, searching on one of the CD products or online databases, and so on.

Susan Dedham always brings her students to the library media center. She is part of the sixth-grade team and teaches language arts to all 125 students on that team. Susan is an avid library user and jointly plans lessons with the library media specialist (LMS). She and Gail Song have worked together for many years. Generally, they plan their lesson about a week before Susan actually brings her classes to the library media center. Gail then prepares a Power Point presentation that introduces the lesson and distributes a handout to the students that will help them work on Susan's current project.

This year, the new standards for English/language arts require that all students at this grade level read at least twenty-five books (or book equivalents). Lakeland Elementary has adopted this standard, and Susan now brings her students every other week to the library media center to select material. Susan and Gail have developed a list of genres that each student will read and report on. Just prior to the students' visit to the library media center, Gail pulls a wide selection of titles from each respective genre for the students to select from. Susan and Gail have jointly developed a series of assessment formats that students may select from, when reporting on their reading. This assessment series allows students to choose: writing alternative endings to a work; writing a letter to the main character; illustrating a pivotal scene from the work; writing to the author about the work; or any one of about twenty-five other options. All students add this report to their portfolio and also write a one-paragraph summary of their thoughts/feelings about the book and why they feel this way.

When the students are actually in the library media center, they select from titles Gail has previewed and pulled from the shelves. Susan then wants the students to read from their selected books, completing at least ten pages before leaving the library media center. Once the children are seated, Gail introduces the genre. This visit, the genre is science fiction. She explains the genre, compares and contrasts it with other genres the children have already read, and gives a brief book talk on about three titles. The children then select their books and begin to read.

Gail moves quietly about the room, advising and guiding the children. Susan pulls out her grade book and begins to call the children individually to her. Gail cannot hear what Susan is saying to the children, but after a few minutes she senses a change in the room. Children are slamming books shut and zipping papers furiously into their backpacks. One girl is crying and two boys have stopped reading and are staring into space with their arms crossed over their chests. Gail moves over to where Susan is seated to see what is going on.

What Gail hears, makes her shudder! Susan is reviewing her paperwork and putting grades into her gradebook. She is calling children over to her who have not done a book report and whose portfolios are incomplete. She is giving each of these children a note home to be signed by their parent or guardian. The letter states that the child's work is incomplete and gives a time line for make-up assignments. Furthermore, Susan assigns each child detention, and the letter informs the parent or guardian of the date that detention is to be served. Gail cannot believe that Susan is using the library media center for this time of chastisement. Gail and her colleagues have worked hard to create a friendly atmosphere. Gail is stopped in her tracks by Susan's behavior. She realizes that if she does not act immediately, there will be four more classes just like this during the day.

Questions

1. Could Gail have anticipated this behavior by Susan?
2. Can Gail stop this before the next class comes in?
3. Should she try?
4. How can she do this and keep her relationship with Susan?
5. What can Gail do now for the children in her room to defuse this situation?
6. Should she try to defuse it?
7. What if Gail does nothing today?
8. Will there be irreparable harm done to the children and to her program?
9. Is it better to hold off and talk with Susan after this event?

THE LIBRARY MEDIA SPECIALIST IS ALSO THE NURSE?

There is no full-time nurse at the Fieldland Middle School. Fieldland is a large middle school with four full-time physical education teachers (all male) and one part-time nurse (female). The nurse's office is located down the hall from the library media center at Fieldland, and both are on the first floor of the building.

Rosario Delosantos is the school nurse teacher at Fieldland. She has extensive experience in working with both elementary and middle school students. Her schedule calls for her to be at Fieldland Middle two full days per week and for one hour on the remaining three days. The one hour is necessary because of the number of children who need medication during the school day. Rosario's other duties are at the elementary school, about two miles away. Rosario is very good about coming to Fieldland and remaining in the event of an emergency. Should she be unavailable during an emergency, the principal, Mr. Lamb, is authorized to call 911.

Tatiana Turlov is the library media specialist at Fieldland Middle School. She describes herself as a "mature woman." She has raised two children of her own, as well as three foster children, and helped to raise several younger siblings after the death of her mother. She is forty-eight years old and has spent the last twelve years at Fieldland. She is highly regarded by her colleagues and her students. She is firm but friendly and will go out of her way to help anyone who asks.

Tatiana opens the library media center early in the morning before school begins and often remains after school, keeping the library media center open for riders of the late bus. She helps students not only with their homework and information needs but also with their recreational reading and interests. In that capacity, she has come to know many of the students who have attended Fieldland over the years, and they often return to visit her. She lives in the community and generally sees three or four of her former students a week as she shops, worships, or attends a community event.

Tatiana has been increasingly concerned with the lack of a full-time nurse at Fieldland. She believes that as a Carnegie Middle School and a participant in the Middle Grade School State Policy Initiative (MGSSPI), there should be a commitment to the eight recommendations of *Turning Points*. Recommendation number six specifically suggests improving academic performance through the fostering of health and fitness of young adolescents. The only health instruction currently offered at Fieldland comes via the four male gym teachers. Health is taught one period a week for each student and consists of them sitting on the floor of the gym and answering some questions en masse about drugs and smoking. There is no specialized instruction related to nutrition, sexually transmitted diseases, AIDS, and pregnancy. Tatiana knows that many students are sexually active, and in the last two semesters she is aware of at least four pregnancies that occurred.

This year Tatiana has been involved in dispensing sanitary products to at least ten sixth-grade girls. The girls go to the nurse's office and find that she is at her other school. They travel on a hall pass that allows them to go only to that office. They can, if they want to chance it, go to the main office, but the secretaries there will not assist them without a correct pass—unless it is an emergency. Clearly, the girls have an emergency situation but certainly not at the 911 level. They could go directly to their sixth-grade assistant principal's office, but he is a male administrator and there are no female ones. At the sixth-grade level, students are quite shy and even uncomfortable asking for sanitary products. A few venture into the library media center, and there they find a welcoming manner, as well as the help they need. Word begins to spread that if you need assistance when the nurse is absent, see the library media specialist. The students are comfortable when they come to see Tatiana because she has established quite a rapport with them. She finally talks with the stock clerk and the nurse and secures a case of sanitary napkins in the library media center closet. She also tells the office secretaries to quietly intervene when younger girls are looking for the nurse and to feel free to send them to her for assistance.

The four male physical-education teachers spend their time in the gym—which is in the basement level and quite a distance from the library media center. Tatiana nonetheless informs them about what she is doing. They are supportive and even provide her with manuals to distribute to the girls who come to her for assistance.

Finally, Tatiana tells all of the grade-level assistant principals and the principal what she is doing. The assistants are relieved that this is one area where they don't need to get involved. The principal, however, is not too happy. He feels that she is overstepping her area of responsibility and working outside of her area of certification. Although he recognizes and appreciates the gap she is filling in the absence of the nurse, he has concerns and asks her to cease and desist until he can get an opinion from the superintendent as to whether or not this should be allowed. Tatiana is quite troubled. She sees the male principal as insensitive to the needs of the women students. She wants him to immediately address the issue of a full-time nurse or else to allow her to continue to provide emergency supplies to the students. She considers taking this matter to both the PTO and the school site-based management team.

Questions

1. Should Tatiana be involved in this matter at all?
2. What recourse does she have? How about the principal?

3. Should Tatiana marshal the forces of the parents and other teachers to address the lack of a full-time nurse in these important grades?
4. How can the school reconcile its participation in the Carnegie Initiative and the MGSSPI with its failure to provide for a full-time nurse? Should the physical education teachers have an active role in this situation?
5. Is Tatiana endangering her certificate by operating outside of the bounds of its confines?

• 5 •

Potholes on the Information Highway

CATALOGING ELECTRONIC/INTERNET RESOURCES

Sadia Mustafa, the school library media specialist at the Woodbury School, had been so excited. She and Dylan McLaughlin, the school's computer teacher, had planned and planned for the day when the school would have resources in the library media center that would go beyond the traditional book and nonautomated, nonprint collection.

Dylan had programs on word processing, graphics, and simple spreadsheet operations in the computer lab. Those were fine for the skills he was responsible for teaching, but both he and Sadia had talked about expanding the research resources for the students in the media center. They had received catalogs and flyers for various electronic encyclopedias and indexes that had many more varied features than the ones already on the shelves. The encyclopedias offered animated graphics, including film clips and sound effects such as speeches, animal sounds, and so on. The indexes provided integrated and Boolean searching techniques for the sources. These resources saved time and effort and, combined with printers, would give students and faculty a great new spectrum of information to access.

Sadia and Dylan had prepared a list of desired titles that they felt should be purchased for the media center. They had included full title, ordering and price information, summaries of contents, and justifications for each entry. They had presented the principal with the list, which had been packaged into a resource bundle. Using the rationale that this purchase would bring the library media center into the next century, the principal had approved the package and the orders had been placed.

Then one day Sadia was reading in one of her journals that some of the resources were now available through the Internet. The article also described some of the Web sites, such as the one that included many of the digitized resources of the Library of Congress, which were available for people to read and print out. It seemed almost as if the entire world was available in electronic format.

The Web sites and other Internet resources were still on Sadia's mind when the first package of electronic programs arrived. As she and Dylan unpacked the encyclopedia and almanac CD-ROM packs, they both realized at the same time that they needed some way to manage these resources. They had ordered computer tables, computers, monitors, and printers and had planned on where to put everything. They had even purchased site licenses for some of the resources and had included a tower for networking the computers.

Perhaps they could print up signs indicating which programs were on which computers. They could put signs on each computer indicating the programs that could be accessed on it. These locational devices would aid users in choosing which computer to use. However, this seemed to be only part of the approach. Sadia felt that access needed to be broadened. Then she thought of a solution. Of course, the titles should be cataloged as part of the online catalog. This would increase user access to subject headings for the various resources and could also include linking notes to other sources.

This seemed to be ideal solution. Now, how to accomplish it? Sadia and Dylan each agreed to do some reading and then meet in two weeks after the CDs had been set up. Sadia concentrated on reading the rule books on cataloging resources and learned that she needed to incorporate special terms and fields into the cataloging record for these new resources. Fortunately, the media center's online catalog had lines already placed on the cataloging templates for the electronic resources, and Sadia just needed to learn what information to place where on the records.

There was also the question of giving classification numbers to the titles. Sadia realized that the electronic media were just another format for the resources of the library media center and that perhaps they should be classified under the same system as the other resources in the center.

Dylan and Sadia both had read about the Internet resources, and Dylan came to the conclusion that it would be a good idea to create a home page for the media center and the computer lab that could be linked to the home page for the school. That way, the students, parents, and teachers could know which resources were where, and it would increase their awareness of the value of the resources.

Sadia, for her part, decided that she could create catalog records that would provide links to the Web sites, which would be valuable resources for the media center users. The links would be part of the cataloging record and would include the name of the Web site and its address, as well as a summary of the contents it accessed.

Both Sadia and Dylan realized that they had quite a project before them, but they felt it would be worthwhile. They both regained their enthusiasm and excitedly started to work on the cataloging and the home page.

Questions

1. Did Sadia and Dylan come up with viable solutions to their perceived problem of access?
2. Should not Sadia and Dylan have planned for the access when they first looked into the idea of electronic and Internet resources?
3. Would a system plan have been useful for identifying the needs for access, as well as the resources themselves?
4. Do you think Sadia and Dylan will also consider a plan for evaluation of the use and access to the new resources? After all, won't they have to justify the acquisition and use of the resources?
5. Is there a need to consider a budget plan for updates and new titles? How should this be done?

ROASTED COMPUTERS

"Here we go again," thought Jasman Bowers, the school library media specialist at the Rahway School, as two students approached her with anguished looks on their faces. They had walked from the computer banks located in the center of the room, and they complained that the computers they were working on had just gone blank.

Jasman calmed the girls down, and all three of them walked over to the computers. The girls showed Jasman which two computers they had been using to find information for their current event reports, and then they noticed that all the other computers in the group had blank screens. Jasman tried to type something on one of the computers, but there was no response. She then tried to reboot the single computer and did the same with each one in the network. Still no result.

Jasman suggested that the students look through some of the periodicals on the magazine rack for information, while she tried to find out what had caused the problem. The girls agreed to do that, and Jasman began to check the wiring connections to make sure they were properly installed and tightly locked in place. All the connections appeared to be fine. Next, Jasman checked the CD tower to be sure that all the disks were properly located. All the proper buttons were lighted, indicating that the tower was operating correctly.

Then Jasman noticed an unusual sound coming from the CPUs (computer processing unit) of the computers. She walked over to one of them and realized that the cooling fan was laboring and making strange whirring noises. Jasman surmised that the problem was overheating of the CPU and the monitor. And no wonder! It was very warm in areas in the school library media center, and Jasman had reported the unevenness of the temperature to the principal, Mr. Javier Cosme, on several occasions. Mr. Cosme had sent the school custodian to check on the temperature/humidity levels of the library media center, and the report had stated that it wasn't that warm in the media center and that nothing needed to be done with the temperature levels.

"Well," thought Jasman. "This time is different." Those computers represented a large investment of money and equipment, and something needed to be done to protect that investment. She remembered a comment one of her library school professors had made to the effect that computers are happiest running in the cold. Action was needed.

Jasman turned off the monitors and the CPUs and asked her aide to cover the library media center while she walked to the office. She found Mr. Cosme and told him of the situation. He realized the validity of her assessment and returned with her to the media center. As he walked in, he agreed that the center was rather warm, and they went over to the computer bank. Jasman turned on a computer, and nothing happened. She then showed Mr. Cosme the properly functioning tower, which was located in a side room that was considerably cooler than the rest of the library media center.

Questions

1. What should Mr. Cosme do next?
2. Along with the computers, do you think the other resources in the library media center could be damaged from the heat?
3. Is air conditioning sufficient, or should the humidity level of the media center also be addressed?
4. Should there be thermometers in the school library media center that could be monitored?

THE HACKER

Hawthorne School was considered to be an ideal educational institution. The school itself was housed in a brand-new building, classrooms were roomy and well equipped for instruction, and the administration was supportive of school personnel. The school library media center was particularly well known for its wealth of resources, helpful staff, and friendly atmosphere.

Among the resources in the library media center were a number of networked computers with access to searching indexes, encyclopedias and other CD-ROM resources, and the Internet. Alberto Rivera, the library media specialist, was particularly proud of the wealth of resources in the library media center and of the way in which students were able to print out information from both print and nonprint sources.

Alberto's library instruction classes stressed information skills, and students always felt confident about doing research at the conclusion of his lessons. It seemed to be an almost-perfect learning situation.

The library was scheduled according to a flexible mode, and many students often came in and out of the library media center during the day. Alberto had a library aide who was in charge of the circulation of library materials on the automated system and who supervised the team of student library helpers who shelved books. This arrangement allowed Alberto to conduct lessons, help students, serve on curriculum committees, plan for speakers, and oversee the computer system.

One day while Alberto was helping a student search for resources on the computer, the system suddenly stopped working. There was no response when Alberto tried to reboot the system. Most of the computers were networked through the tower in the office, but some were stand-alones or two tied together to share a resource. Alberto checked the tower and it seemed to be functioning properly. He returned to the computer bank and walked around to the computer stations. All the computers had students sitting in front of them, apparently waiting for the computers to resume working. All the computers, that is, except the one that Sean Feisner was using. Sean seemed to be typing away on some database, and that seemed unusual.

When Alberto approached Sean to ask him what he was working on, Sean had a worried expression on his face. He looked up at Alberto and in a very small voice stated that he had accidentally accessed the files and had mistakenly caused the system to crash. He had been searching for some resources and had mistakenly pushed some buttons that he believed were not to be used for the commands with which he was working. Alberto could hardly believe his ears: Could all those resources possibly be damaged? How could it have been an accident? These and other questions whirled around in his mind as he heard Sean's words. Now what to do?

Questions

1. Do you believe it was an accident?
2. Could Sean have affected all the computers, considering that they were not all networked to the same tower?
3. Do you think Sean was a "hacker" who deliberately crashed the files?
4. What should happen to Sean?

IT IS ALL PART OF THE JOB—OR IS IT?

Sam Jerome is a new sixth-grade teacher at the St. Brendan's Academy. This school offers a preparatory program for students in the middle grades. It is an independent school with a focus on mathematics and science. The faculty members are skilled practitioners who emphasize integration across all subject areas. The teachers and students work together to construct meaning for their assignments, which are based in the "real world."

All faculty members are fully certified by the state and hold certification in two related areas, such as math/science or language arts/social science. Sam holds a language arts/geography certificate with a middle school and an ESL endorsement. He teaches both language arts and social sciences to his sixth-graders and expects to "loop" with them for the next two years.

St. Brendan's Academy requires that the students have access at home to a computer. The school has a Web page that allows students and parents to check on individual progress across subject areas. Students regularly e-mail their homework to their instructors, and parents communicate with teachers and one another about the class work. St. Brendan's has a high-speed line, two computer labs operating in a Windows environment, pods throughout the facility, and a fully up-to-date library media center. Within the library media center, separated by a glass wall, is another computer lab that is used for Internet searching as well as word processing, publishing, and so on.

The library media specialist at St. Brendan's is Natalia Cruz. Natalia has been a school library media specialist for about five years. Prior to coming to St. Brendan's last year, she was at a public middle school in another town. Natalia was hired at St. Brendan's after what the headmaster calls an "intergalactic search." In truth, Natalia was required to have two certifications and that proved a hard combination to find. Natalia has not only library media certification but also a business certificate. In addition, she has an ESL endorsement and a middle-school endorsement. Natalia prides herself on her ability to function well in the high-tech world of St. Brendan's Academy. In correspondence with her colleagues across the state, she tells them she works in "library media heaven."

Natalia was asked during her interview to describe her strengths and weaknesses. She told the panel that her strengths were her ability to function effectively and efficiently in a changing technological world. Her weakness, she said, was her difficulty in accepting that others are not on the same comfort level with technology as she is. The panel felt that this was a weakness with which they could certainly live. Natalia was hired and is now in her second year at St. Brendan's. She spent most of the first year getting to know the students, faculty, and parents and, of course, the collection. She would like a print collection of about 10,000 volumes and is working hard with the faculty and staff at mapping the collection to determine weaknesses and strengths. The headmaster has confidence in Natalia's abilities but is somewhat concerned about her personal interactions with the staff. She is extremely patient with the students but conveys to the staff an attitude of superiority that often borders on rudeness.

Sam Jerome is not as technologically savvy as Natalia. He can surf the Net but has difficulty formatting a search strategy. Sam is not as experienced a teacher as Natalia, and he does have some classroom-management difficulties. Each month, Sam schedules his classes into the library media center. He always has his students reading and then writing about what they read. The writings may involve variant endings, character studies, expansions along personal lines of themes found in the readings, and so on. Each writing is saved in an electronic portfolio. The students add to their portfolios over the course of the school year. It is Sam's plan, since he will "loop" with his students, that their electronic portfolios comprise the results of three years' of work. When Sam's students come to the library media center each month to search for a new book to read, he also expects them to work in the computer lab.

Although the lab is scheduled separately from the library media center, Natalia oversees it—loading software, running virus scans, maintaining printers. Natalia checks the lab in the media center on a regular basis but generally has relatively little to do to maintain it. Teachers who bring their classes to the library media center and the lab are generally proficient in diagnosing and solving any difficulties that arise. Natalia has noticed, however, that teachers who have difficulty managing their classes have many more difficulties when in the lab. Natalia cringes when Sam's students work on the computers in the lab. She always has to spend considerable time in the lab after he and his students are finished. The difficulties range from unplugged monitors and mice to uninstalled printers, long printer queues with the printers turned off to stop the queue, and frozen keyboards.

At the end of his class today, Sam comes to Natalia while his students are lining up in the hall. He gives her a list (written on scrap paper) of difficulties he encountered at each workstation. The list is just too extensive and Natalia explodes. She was counting on leaving school on time today, as she has a long-standing dental appointment. Instead, at five minutes to dismissal she is presented with a list of stupid errors. Sam could have prevented most of them by managing his students better, and the rest he should have been able to correct himself. Natalia, in front of Sam's assembled students, asks him why there are so many problems when he and his classes are in the lab. She asks him why he waited until he had such a list instead of summoning her when the first problem arose. She continues in a shrill voice to tell him that she is tired of having to pick up after him and his students and she is tired of doing the jobs of others. She is not the computer repairman or woman, and she slams the door in Sam's face.

Questions

1. What can be done to repair the damage Natalia has done by blowing up in front of Sam and his students?
2. Is it Natalia's job to maintain the lab that is adjacent to the library media center?
3. Should St. Brendan's have a clearly stated policy about teacher competency in using a lab with a group of students?
4. Should Natalia work with teachers before they schedule their classes into the lab so that issues that are unique to working in a machine room are dealt with before they become critical?

WHO IS MINDING THE STUDENTS IN THE LAB?

At St. Brendan's Academy the faculty members are abuzz about the blow-up between Natalia Cruz, the school library media specialist, and Sam Jerome, the sixth-grade language arts and social studies teacher. Even the students are talking about how Natalia really yelled at Sam. The headmaster has met with Natalia and told her how unprofessional her behavior was. He has given her a written reprimand, which he has placed in her personnel folder.

Natalia cannot believe that she behaved the way she did. She is absolutely mortified. She writes a note to Sam asking if she can speak with him privately. He agrees and she apologizes profusely. She asks him if she can speak with his students, and he agrees to that as well. Natalia goes to his classroom, shuts the door, and tries to explain to the children about losing her cool. She tells them that she was wrong and just exploded because she was feeling overworked and underappreciated. She does a good job of presenting her case, and the students learn much about handling conflict from her explanation.

Natalia treads softly during the next few months. She tries to be more tolerant toward the staff members with their technology concerns and makes a point of being gracious to Sam. Eventually, the staff and students stop murmuring about her behavior. Natalia has learned a valuable lesson by publicly embarrassing herself. She relives that moment in the hall with Sam countless times in her mind and resolves to never lose control like that again. The issue of who is responsible for the lab within the library media center continues to be one with which Natalia wrestles.

She has developed a program for upkeep of the computers around the building. Since there is no computer teacher, no one seems to be in charge of maintaining the equipment. Using her "tech troops," Natalia provides minor diagnostic and repair services around the building. The students who comprise the "tech troops" are skilled in the rudiments of changing printer drivers and cartridges, installing software, scanning files for viruses, and so on. The time spent in training these students has been well worth the effort. Now, even when a teacher with weak management skills has difficulties in one of the labs, the "tech troops" can handle the problems. Because the "tech troops" come from across teams and grades, there is almost one in every class. This, by itself, reduces the number of times that Natalia is summoned for emergency computer repair.

As the school year winds to a close, Natalia begins to notice a pattern of unscheduled, "emergency" use of the lab within the library media center. Once again, it comes from a sixth-grade teacher. Ross Rosala teaches math and science to the same team of sixth-graders as

Sam Jerome. Ross is very competent with technology and has an Internet pod both in his classroom and in his science lab. His students research, write, and edit their lab work, using the machines in one of the pods. Ross moves effortlessly back and forth between his science lab and his science classroom. The work in the two rooms is seamlessly interwoven. Natalia admires his ease in managing his students in both venues.

Ross has essentially closed out his science lab for the year. The regional and state science fairs have been held, and statewide science testing has recently been completed. Less than thirty days are left in the school year, and Ross has decided to keep his students in his science classroom. He is still providing them with challenging work, and they continue to use his classroom pod for Internet searching, word processing, and the like. Because the science lab is closed, his students do not have access to the computer pod located there. Ross begins to send four or five students every day to the school library media center. Since there are thirty seats in the lab inside the media center, he feels no need to schedule the students ahead of time. He simply calls Natalia, tells her he just needs a few students to have access, and sends them down to the lab.

Natalia often has groups of students in both the library media center proper and the lab, but since teachers accompany those students, supervision is never an issue. Lately, with Ross Rosala's students coming in unsupervised and a full complement of students in the library proper coming in and out in small groups with a pass, Natalia begins to worry about the lack of proper supervision of all students. St. Brendan's does have an acceptable use policy in effect, but Natalia notices that Ross's students are often not entirely focused on their research or word processing. She also begins to resent that she has five or six students every day from Ross's classes whom she is watching. Sometimes they come in and seem to be pretty unfocused. Often the students who come from Ross's class are those whom Natalia feels need close supervision.

Natalia begins to feel that Ross is taking advantage of her. Although there are always enough seats in the lab to accommodate the students, they do need some supervision. If no one is in the library media center or the lab, Natalia cannot even run out to the bathroom or to check her mail in the office. She cannot leave these students alone. Given her past history with the sixth-grade team, Natalia is loathe to say anything to Ross, and so the situation continues until the school year comes to a close.

Questions

1. Is this a problem, or is Natalia just being overly sensitive because of her past difficulties with Sam Jerome?
2. If the lab is separated from the library media center proper by a glass wall, is it really Natalia's domain?
3. So what if Natalia has to keep an eye on Ross's students and misses her chance to get her mail or a cup of coffee?
4. Are there real issues of liability and responsibility here?
5. What if something happened to a student on the other side of the glass wall and Natalia was busy working in the library media center and could not maintain a line of sight perspective?
6. How should Natalia approach this situation when the school year starts anew?

SMUT IN THE MIDDLE SCHOOL

Alex Melosian works full time at the Plaza Middle School. He is an older man who spent many years in corporate libraries. He made the shift to school library media specialist when his children went to college. He always wanted to work with young people, and he was able to take an early retirement from the corporation where he worked. Alex brings a great many competencies to his present work environment. Because he is older and a man, the students tend to be more respectful. He is a hard worker and tackles his job with a tremendous amount of enthusiasm and humor. No task is too large or small; no request for information or instruction is left unmet.

Alex is faced with trying to bring his nineteenth-century school library media center into the twenty-first century. Things he took for granted in the corporate world are just not found in the world of schools. He has asked for a faculty committee to advise him on balancing the needs of the print and electronic collection. He has also taken the initiative in bringing in technology. He started with a Technology Plan and from that will flow all requests for high-speed lines, online catalogs, scanners, Web page design, and so on. Because Alex came from the corporate world, he has many contacts to call upon for needed advice and service. By the end of Alex Melosian's first year on the job, he has accomplished a great deal. He has weeded the collection, replaced the computers with local funding, installed a high-speed line using grant monies, and begun to create an online catalog. He knows that for the coming year, things will be in a state of flux as he arranges for e-mail accounts for all of the faculty members, trains people in the use of search engines, gets AUPs set up for everyone, and continues to work on the online catalog. With only one clerical assistant, Alex is busy indeed.

The second year opens with a sense of awe and wonder on the part of the faculty. So much has been done in the library media center in so little time. Alex is thrilled, and so are the faculty and students. Alex holds his open house for new and returning faculty members to explain to them what is going on. He tells them about the e-mail accounts and announces a training schedule for using them and for Internet searching. At the end of the session, a new faculty member introduces himself. His name is Gaetano Silvia. He is a science teacher newly assigned to Plaza Middle School. He is a substitute, but since he is science-certified, he feels confident that he will be here for the entire school year. Alex is pleased to work with a new teacher and offers to help him in any way possible.

Gaetano tells Alex that he has a list of sites he would like bookmarked or saved on the computers so that students may quickly and easily go to them. The sites are specific to the work the students will be doing this first quarter. Alex spends the next afternoon saving the sites to the ten workstations in the school library media center. Gaetano brings his students to the center, and the two men begin to explain how the sites work, describe what will be happening during the coming quarter, and also begin to touch on search engines. Alex is quick to keep an eye on the students, as he has not yet developed AUPs. The students are so eager to see what Gaetano and Alex have done that they are not interested in surfing the Net on their own.

Chapter 5

Over the new two weeks, Gaetano brings all of his classes to the school library media center several times. Each time, he and Alex work as a team to introduce the sites, search engines, and so on. Alex is thrilled to have such an enthusiastic and knowledgeable colleague.

In early October, Gaetano comes to the library media center during his planning time. He tells Alex that he is going to use his AOL account to check his e-mail and to search new sites for the next quarter. Alex is busy with a class and he just nods to Gaetano. Gaetano uses one of the workstations on the high-speed line that has AOL installed on it. He spends a few minutes there and then comes over and asks Alex for a favor, saying that he has forgotten his password on AOL and cannot get into his account. Alex replies, "No problem;" he will set Gaetano up using his own account. Alex goes over and types in his account name and password—Gaetano averts his eyes so that he does not violate Alex's privacy. Alex tells Gaetano that he is all set and resumes working with the class. The class that Alex is working with will be in the library media center for a double period. The students are busy researching, printing, taking notes, and so on. Alex is quite busy with them, as is their classroom teacher. After about forty minutes Alex notices that Gaetano is still at the computer. He goes over and sees that Gaetano is in the romance chatroom. Alex is furious and tells Gaetano to get off the line. Gaetano says not to worry, "I told them I was using a friend's account so they know it isn't you writing." The next day Alex receives three X-rated e-mail messages. Each day he gets at least five and he doesn't know how to stop them.

Questions

1. What was Alex thinking when he let Gaetano use his e-mail address/account?
2. Did Gaetano break any laws when he checked into chat rooms using a school computer and on school time?
3. How can Alex stop getting X-rated e-mails?
4. Why didn't Alex just get Gaetano onto the high-speed line where he could check out his sites and leave the e-mail to be checked at home, later?
5. Should the library media center have a written policy about Internet use by the faculty, including chat rooms?

THE DISTRICT CUT OUT THE MAGAZINES

Each elementary school in the Central Lake District gets a flat allotment from the Department of Teaching and Learning for periodical purchases. All of the paperwork for these requests is filled out centrally, with appropriate mailing addresses included so that the periodicals are mailed directly to the school library media centers. Each elementary school, regardless of size, reading or interest level, special program, or focus, receives $200 from this flat allotment. Every spring each of the district's school library media specialists is sent a list of what was purchased for the collection the previous year. It is for information purposes only, not to be revised, updated, or edited. The $200 generally buys between eight and ten journal titles. The titles are those that are generally found in an elementary school, such as *Appleseeds, Cricket, Sports Illustrated for Kids,* and the like.

Marty Perrone is the school library media specialist at the Hawthorne Elementary School. Hawthorne has an enrollment of 500 students in grades K through 5. The school receives Magnet funds and focuses on the performing arts. Marty has access to Magnet funding for print and nonprint resources but finds that purchasing periodicals is often cumbersome. For the last several years he has relied upon the monies provided by the Department of Teaching and Learning to fund his periodicals. He has been busy with his collection development focus in other areas and has been somewhat content to maintain the status quo. As more and more of his time is spent on research, however, Marty finds that he wants to add to his periodical collection. He feels that he needs to subscribe to *Odyssey* for the science teacher and her class and also to *Cobblestone* for the fourth and fifth grades. He would like to get a few professional periodicals, as well, especially some like *Educational Leadership* or maybe *Kappan*. A host of children's magazines would support Hawthorne's focus on the performing arts, and Marty also gradually wants to add those to the collection.

Marty feels strongly that he needs to supplement his print collection with electronic databases and periodical titles. He thinks that the present budget is way too small and doesn't begin to meet the needs of special-focus schools like Hawthorne. Marty talks with several of his colleagues across the city and is quite surprised by what he discovers. It seems that the Department of Teaching and Learning only sets aside money for the elementary schools. That small amount is nothing compared to what the middle and high schools receive from their principals' budgets. One high school spends over $2,500 on periodicals in both print and electronic format. Even the middle schools receive about $1,500 from their principals. Marty is fuming. He makes an appointment to see the director of Teaching and Learning.

Dr. Johanna Maloney is the director, and she has only been on the job for three months. She is barely aware of this funding issue. She does tell Marty, however, that she feels that the inequities in the present system can be corrected by getting more money from the principal's budget. Marty has already had that discussion with his principal—and it has gone nowhere. The principals feel stretched and think that the central office should support this component of teaching and learning. Johanna tells Marty that there is no more money coming from central office—in fact, the periodical budget is being cut by 60 percent in the central office, and that includes the Department of Teaching and Learning. Marty tells Johanna that he will consult with his fellow elementary colleagues about a course of action.

Within two weeks, Marty and the other elementary school library media specialists are notified that because the central office periodical budget has been cut by 60 percent, the Office of Teaching and Learning will no longer support subscriptions at the schools. Marty is livid. He feels that this unfairly penalizes the elementary school library media specialists but has no impact on those at the middle and high school. Marty feels that the elementary school library media specialists are taking a double hit. First, the school year is already underway and the expected purchases that were cut leave a gap that cannot be filled in the middle of a budget year. Second, Marty and his colleagues feel that Dr. Maloney is too new on the job to focus her attention on this rather small budget issue. They decide to get together and file a grievance across the district regarding the inequities of the periodical budget process. At the meeting, the sixteen elementary school library media specialists discuss what they want as a solution to the cut—do they want the $200 per school that they previously had? Perhaps they should keep the budget monies the same but retain selection rights? Since the money is the same across all of the elementary schools and there is a variation in size and focus at the schools, should there be a per-head allotment? Where do electronic databases fit into this mix? The group forms a subcommittee to study the issues and get back to the whole group with a recommended solution to this dilemma.

Questions

1. Is a grievance the answer to this problem? What are the ramifications for library media specialists in filing a "class action" grievance such as this one?
2. What are some solutions to the inequities? Are there really inequities or have the middle- and high-school library media specialists done a better job of promoting their services to their principals and buildings?
3. Do large periodical collections and electronic databases belong in elementary schools?
4. Do/can elementary school students really do research that would involve using periodicals and electronic databases?
5. Should the library media specialists be able to select the periodicals for their own collections?

II

BIGGER ISSUES: PLANNING, POLICIES, AND PERSONNEL

• 6 •

Certification

PARAPROFESSIONAL VOLUNTEERS

It was not that Isra Ibrahim was an excellent volunteer. It was not that he was such a great help to Gloria. It was not even the fact that Isra served as a substitute when Gloria Caraballo, the school library media specialist at Austin School, was absent. There was something else, and Gloria could not quite fathom what the element was that rattled around in the back of her mind.

Isra was Gloria's excellent aide. He was a paraprofessional with a college degree in English who worked at home as a writer and had time for about fifteen hours a week to help out at the library media center as a volunteer. The school's administration had told Gloria about five years ago that there was no money for a salaried aide to help in the library media center. As a consequence, Gloria had asked for volunteers through an article in the school's newspaper that was distributed to students and parents.

Several parents, Isra among them, had responded, and now only Isra was still there in the media center. His children had left the school, but Isra enjoyed the time in the library and willingly helped out whenever he could. On occasion, he even stayed more than the fifteen hours he had set for volunteer work.

Isra was the organizer of the library club and planned the work schedules of the students. He trained them, checked their work, and frequently rewarded them for excellent performance with homemade cookies that his wife baked as a treat. The library media center was always neat and organized because of Isra's efforts with the library club.

When Gloria organized a school visit from a children's author, Isra was the one who wrote the publicity articles, prepared the programs for the presentation, and set up the cookies and punch for the after-program refreshments. He even visited the local library and gathered information about the visiting author from the series "Something about the Author." Gloria was very pleased with all his efforts and publicly thanked him at the close of the program.

As a follow-up to the author's visit, Gloria suggested to Isra that he present a program for the school, based upon his own writing. Isra was uneasy about the idea, since his writing was for adults and covered nonfiction topics. Gloria pointed out that it would be very valuable for the students to see how Isra researched his topics and then put the ideas into his own words so that they would be understandable for others to learn from. She felt that it would reinforce the information and research skills she was teaching the students in her library instruction sessions and would be an inspiration for those students.

Isra liked Gloria's rationale, and they set a date for the presentation. Isra designed the program using graphics he found on a computer program and included quotes from some of his work and an outline of his research and writing work routine. His wife promised extra-special refreshments for the occasion, and his children volunteered to make some supporting remarks on how important research was to the writing process. It seemed as if the only thing that was lacking was a musical introduction, but Gloria and Isra agreed that music was not really necessary.

The day before the program Gloria finally realized what had been bothering her about Isra's role as a paraprofessional volunteer. With all the duties that Isra had assumed to help Gloria in her work with the curriculum, selection of materials, and organization of the library media center, he was almost a school library media specialist himself.

Since Isra was a volunteer, Gloria had not asked him for a résumé. He had mentioned that he had time to volunteer since he worked at home, and that was enough for her. She never thought about the fact that he seemed to be almost a natural teacher who worked well with students and had a knack for instructing as he trained. It occurred to Gloria that he might be a certified teacher who should be encouraged to work for his school library educational media specialist certificate.

Questions

1. What should Gloria do next?
2. Should paraprofessional volunteers be, at the very least, certified teachers?
3. Was it proper for Isra to substitute for Gloria if he was not a certified teacher? Since library media specialists are, in a sense, teachers who are assigned to the library media center, should not their replacements be similarly certified?
4. What do you think of Gloria's idea of having Isra as a guest speaker? Was her rationale sensible?

HERE COMES THE SUPERVISOR

Destinee Boyona sat at her desk and re-read the letter for the fourth time. She stared at the print, asking herself what should she do? The request in the letter seemed simple enough, but Destinee wondered what would come next. She had been the school library media specialist in the Roxbury School for ten years, and this was the first time she had received such a letter.

The principal of the school had forwarded the letter to Destinee, with a note clipped to it that told her to handle the matter any way she wished. Destinee knew that it was useless to consult the principal for advice, based upon the attitude expressed in his note, so she finally decided to call her friend, the media specialist in the middle school.

When Judy answered the phone in the middle school library media center, she was surprised at the almost-panicked tone of Destinee's voice. Judy quickly agreed to meet Destinee for a cup of coffee after school at a local cafe, and they set 4:00 as the time for their meeting.

Destinee felt some relief in knowing that help would soon be at hand, and she proceeded to teach encyclopedia-searching skills to two classes in the afternoon. When the final bell of the day rang, she straightened up the media center and then left to meet Judy.

It was a rainy afternoon, and the cups of coffee the two women ordered were comforting. After taking a few sips, Destinee showed the letter to Judy, who responded to the text with a delighted smile. Destinee had been asked if she would be willing to serve as a supervisor for Derion Ayala, a student who was taking the field experience course in the local college's educational media program and had asked to be placed in the Roxbury School. Attached to the letter was a form that indicated that Destinee would need to certify that the student had completed certain activities and skills and that Destinee would be handsomely compensated for her work with the student.

Judy indicated that she was rather jealous of Destinee for this wonderful opportunity. Destinee responded to Judy with the concern that she was not sure what to do as a supervisor and that perhaps she should recommend that the student be placed with Judy instead. Judy rejected that suggestion and told Destinee that she should be proud of this offer and that now they should sit and cooperatively plan what Destinee should do.

Judy's confidence in Destinee had the desired effect: Destinee now settled into concrete positive thoughts on the steps she should follow for this big experience. Together, they outlined a plan of action, commencing with a letter of acceptance to the college's field experience office and a request for more details regarding its expectations of her and information about the student.

They then decided to look at the skills that were expected to be mastered by the student and tried to think of ways that he could be exposed to them. Derion's name seemed familiar to Destinee, and she suddenly remembered why. Derion had been a student in the Roxbury School and had worked as a student aide in the library media center. She was pleased that Derion had decided to become a school library media specialist, and she wanted to be the best supervisor she could for him.

Derion would have an advantage, in that he had some experience in the school library media center. Destinee began to remember back to the time when she had decided to become a media specialist after teaching in another town for a number of years. She had felt the need for variety in her activities and had wanted to expand her horizons. The school library media center seemed to be the perfect place to satisfy her wishes.

And so it had probably been for Derion. With a start, Destinee realized that she had been off in another world and had been neglecting Judy. Judy was saying that Destinee could remind Derion of the activities he had undertaken as a student aide and that now he would be going beyond those duties. She also reminded Destinee that Derion had probably been exposed to many of the skills in his classes in the college, and the field experience should be a culminating practice for him.

Questions

1. What should Destinee do next after writing to the college?
2. Should the principal be informed of Destinee's decision?
3. What role should the principal play in the upcoming field experience?
4. What skills do you think Derion should master?
5. How much do you think Derion will have learned in classes prior to his field experience? Is it a matter of applying practicality to philosophy?

THE BIG RELICENSING ISSUE

Edwin Acevado had been the school library media specialist at Hillside School for five years. He was a tenured member of the faculty and held a master's degree in education, with a concentration in educational media. Edwin had built up the school library media center with a well-rounded collection of print and nonprint materials and had worked on the development of the automated resources and systems. It seemed as if Edwin had his career well in hand.

Edwin's mood of complacency was rather rudely broken when, at the staff meeting on Wednesday afternoon, the principal, Amanda Garcia, announced to all faculty members that the relicensing period had come around again, and that faculty who had been in the five-year cycle needed to prepare for plans to renew their licenses. Mrs. Garcia stated that the affected personnel would need to submit personal improvement plans, or PIPs, on how they would comply with the state regulations that required staff members to show professional growth in order to maintain and renew their certifications.

This requirement was news to Edwin, who had never heard of it before. He joined the other faculty members who were neophytes in asking Mrs. Garcia what would be involved in this plan. She announced that she would prepare some materials on the process and hold a special faculty meeting for those who needed more information.

When the day of the special meeting arrived, Edwin and his fellow relicensing candidates joined Amanda Garcia in the teachers' lounge and looked at the packets of materials she handed to them. They were all amazed at the range of activities that had been marked as possible items for the plans. The approved items ranged from attendance at conferences to taking classes at the local college. There were also ideas for workshops, for writing, and for presentations at meetings. Some in-house workshops were also included on the list. Along with the approved ideas was a list of unacceptable items that would not count toward the improvement plan.

All this seemed rather intimidating to Edwin and his colleagues, and the first question they asked Amanda pertained to the format of the personal improvement plan. Her response was that they each needed to put in writing exactly what they intended to do for the plan and that each activity must relate to the overall subject objective of their plan. That comment also raised questions, for this was the first time they had heard anything about specific objectives.

After calming down their cries of consternation, Mrs. Garcia put on her principal's hat and informed the faculty members that their plans were to be personal improvement plans and this implied that an area of their content or skills needed improvement or development. She urged them all to assess their areas of instruction and decide upon something that could be used as a goal for improvement. Then, the next step would be to identify the types of activities that would be useful for this development. She reminded them that this plan was mandatory and that it should be geared toward something that would be useful and beneficial to their teaching and their licenses. She hinted that the use of automation in some form or other might be a good area for a plan.

Edwin returned to the school library media center and decided to put on his thinking cap. The media center was already automated, but Edwin began to focus his thoughts upon the comments he had heard students express when they had difficulty finding the information they needed for reports. Suddenly, he had an inspiration: he would develop his plan around the installation of and instruction in the use of the Internet on the library's computers.

Questions

1. What type of approved activities do you think would be appropriate for Edwin's plan?
2. What should be the essential elements in Edwin's plan?
3. Does Edwin need to learn about the Internet before he goes about learning how to install it through the school for the library's computers?
4. Would Edwin need to involve other people in his project, or do you think he could do it himself? If he did include other people, would he be the director of the project in a manner that would satisfy the need for the plan to be for his personal improvement?

EMERGENCY CERTIFICATION

It was already February 1st, and Tremell Edwards was wondering what to do next. He had served as the school library media specialist in the Burry School with emergency certification. He had been in this position ever since the former media specialist had left. Tremell, a former fifth-grade teacher, had been appointed by the principal, Ahmed Salem, to the title when there were no qualified applicants to fill the vacancy.

Dr. Salem had applied for the emergency certification status for Tremell and had shown him the regulations that required Tremell to take three courses in educational media per year. Tremel agreed to do this and was enthusiastic about the appointment and the classwork.

The work in the school library media center was challenging and Tremell discovered that he was quite adept with the computers and in installing the automated system. He had been an English major, with an elementary education minor in college, and his background in literature and English skills served him well as he entered records into the online catalog and circulation system. Book talks became one of the staples of his library program, and he coaxed students into reading many different types of literature.

Tremell found it hard to imagine being anywhere else in the school other than inside the library media center. He developed bulletin boards and displays, he produced a newsletter of library happenings, and he staged two plays about library cats and mice. Tremell felt that he was really in his element.

The classwork was also stimulating. Tremell's instructors geared their assignments around the various activities in the school library media center, and Tremell culled a number of ideas to use in his media center from class discussions. Tremell felt that he was receiving a good solid foundation for his role as a school library media specialist.

It was in one of his classes that spring semester that Tremell's instructor mentioned that students who were approaching the end of their eligibility for preliminary certification via the emergency route needed to make some decisions. The emergency route was designed to cover the employment of staff members as they obtained the first stage of certification. Full certification as educational media specialist was awarded only after students had completed the requirements for a master's degree.

An acting media specialist could continue to serve in the media center as long as a fully certified candidate did not apply for the position. Tremell could "guarantee" his job only if he continued his education and "locked out" any competition. Tremell looked over the course descriptions of the courses he would need to complete for the master's degree. Although he had enjoyed the courses that related directly to the library media center, he was not as sure he would like the education-type courses and, especially, the thesis courses.

Tremell now knew what the instructor meant when he stated that the students would need to make some decisions. He felt that the time had come when he should talk to Dr. Salem, who had put him in this position in the first place. Tremell made an appointment to see Dr. Salem for a serious discussion. They looked over the catalog and analyzed each course that Tremell might take. When Tremell mentioned his reservations about the thesis requirement, Ahmed reassured him that the research would not be too onerous (he spoke from personal experience) and that he would receive plenty of help from his colleagues at the school when he needed a group as a pilot and final study subject. Tremell felt better, but he still had some reservations.

Questions

1. What do you think Tremell's decision will be?
2. Would this be an opportunity for Tremell to brush up on his English background and apply it to the media center in an academic exercise?
3. Why is it important for full certification to be connected to the master's degree? Is this similar to other certifications in other fields?
4. Can you think of any subjects that Tremell might choose to incorporate into his thesis if he decides to seek full certification?

GROW YOUR OWN SCHOOL LIBRARY MEDIA SPECIALIST

Since 1987, the Centerville Regional School District has had no fewer than ten full-time library media specialist vacancies among its forty-plus elementary schools. A variety of reasons exist for this critical staffing shortage. First of all, there is a residency requirement. Any employee of the district must move into the county within six months of hire. He or she must produce an affidavit of residency, along with three other proofs—phone bill, utility bill, tax statement, and so on. Some people do move into the county; some provide falsified information; but most just apply to other districts in the region.

The second reason that the critical staffing shortage exists has to do with the nature of the jobs at the schools. Each of the affected schools has a 90 percent free lunch rate. This means that the schools have 90 percent of their students living at or below the national poverty rate. This element of risk among the students is often translated into low test scores, increased amounts of truancy, low attendance rates, and a greater need for social services at the school. Many teachers simply choose not to work in an environment with this type of student.

The third and final reason for the staffing shortage has to do with the library media centers themselves. All of the affected schools require that the school library media specialist operate on a fixed schedule of classes. This is combined with bus and lunch duties on a daily basis. Since the schools have been unstaffed for two or more years, the collections are in disarray and have no computer access of any type.

Bobbie and Grace are two school library media specialists in Centerville. Both have been hired from outside of the area. Both have husbands whose work has brought them to the region, and both are invigorated by the challenges offered in Centerville. Both have developed successful programs and often mentor newer library media specialists, as well as supervise practicum students from the local graduate library school. Bobbie and Grace have been school library media specialists for about twelve years and have worked in several districts around the United States. Because of their experience, principals often call upon them to provide some guidance for the substitutes assigned to the schools with school library media specialists. They are also hired by the district to complete the book orders and inventory that are mandated by the state for these unstaffed facilities. These activities are generally done during the summer months, and extra compensation is involved.

Bobbie and Grace are hard workers at their own school library media centers and appreciate the opportunities to work during the summer months. They are troubled, however, by what they see during the summer at the schools where the staffing is temporary. The school library media centers at those schools are in total disarray. Hundreds of books are missing; the card catalogs are not maintained; the shelves contain damaged books and are in no particular order. Both women know that no level of quality library media service is provided to the children or teachers at these schools.

After agonizing over the staffing program, Bobbie and Grace come up with an idea. They know that plenty of substitutes get assigned to "cover" the library media centers. Why not develop a training program for these teachers? After brainstorming this idea with some other school library media specialists, they refine their idea even more. Why not offer the positions to these substitutes on a permanent basis? Perhaps they would be interested in becoming school library media specialists and leave the classroom behind? They would be provided with a formal training program, a long-term mentoring program, and a permanent position with a full benefit package. In exchange, these new school library media specialists would be required to complete six credits annually in the graduate library program at the university, eventually earning an MLS.

After a summer of negotiating with the bargaining unit and the Human Resources Office of the Centerville Regional School District, Bobbie and Grace receive the go-ahead to contact the Certification Department of the state. With its knowledge of the staffing shortage at Centerville, the State Certification Department is open to a creative way to staff these chronic long-term vacancies. It agrees to provide emergency certificates based upon the prior classroom teaching experience of the candidates, an existing valid classroom-teaching certificate, and continuous training provided by the district. Furthermore, the Certification Department stipulates that these newly certified school library media specialists must successfully complete six graduate library-school credits by the end of the school year. Within five years they must complete all degree requirements for the MLS.

Bobbie and Grace, along with the director of human resources, interview the candidates. The three identify twelve candidates for this new staffing initiative, which is called "Grow Your Own School Library Media Specialist." All twelve participate in the training and mentoring efforts sponsored by the district, are permanently hired, and enroll in the graduate library program. They report to their new library media centers effective with the second semester of the school year. Bobbie and Grace receive great feedback from the principals and teachers at the schools where the new library media specialists are placed. What's not to love about permanent staff members who are trained and mentored by experienced and enthusiastic colleagues? Bobbie and Grace continue to meet with the "fledglings," as they become known. These meetings are biweekly and offer training in classroom/library connections, storytelling tips, and so on.

Eventually, a problem is vocalized—the graduate courses at the university are not what the "fledglings" expect. They feel ostracized by the faculty in the graduate school, and one particular faculty member seems to single them out for ridicule during classes. They also feel that when they present a sample lesson in class, tell a story, or complete a project, they are held to a different standard than other students. They are often referred to as the "herd" or "the wannabes." The twelve people experience a general discouragement over their commitment to the MLS Program. Several talk openly about their frustration, which is rapidly turning to anger. They feel that other, less experienced students have an easier time of it in the graduate classroom. Bobbie and Grace are troubled by this perception. They worry that the "fledglings" will drop out and return to the classroom. Then, Centerville will be back where it started.

Bobbie and Grace decide that they should meet with the dean of the Graduate Library School. They also decide to meet with the director of the School Library Media Program there. They will share their concerns with both individuals and hope for the best.

Questions

1. Is it possible that the problem at the university stems from their not being included in the early discussions about this program?
2. Should a representative from the university have been included in the developmental stage of this program, as the university will be providing the graduate coursework essential to the long-range success of this program?
3. Is it possible that the fledglings, traveling as a group through the graduate program, intimidate their professors as well as the other students?
4. Should Bobbie and Grace have foreseen this problem?
5. Is it possible that the fledglings hold some responsibility for this difficulty?
6. Is this program a viable one to solving a critical shortage area?

7. Would this shortage problem be eliminated if there were no residency requirement?
8. Would it be eliminated if the elementary schools in question had flexible schedules with greater access to technology?
9. What impact does 90 percent free lunch have on the short- and long-term success of this problem?

EMERGENCY CERTIFICATE = HARASSMENT?

Emilio Vargas is halfway through his graduate program at the University. He wants to become a school library media specialist, but the coursework is difficult. In addition, Emilio has family obligations—a wife and three small children. His job as a teacher's assistant just does not pay enough to sustain his family, and Emilio has borrowed heavily to pay for his graduate work.

Emilio is the first in his family to receive a college degree. He majored in social studies and received a teaching certificate as a secondary teacher. Unfortunately, there are no permanent positions as secondary social studies teachers in the greater geographic area. Since substitute teaching pays so little, Emilio takes a full-time job with the Plainview School Department as a teacher's assistant in a self-contained middle-school special education room. The pay is steady, and the job includes a complete benefit package. Emilio regards this as temporary employment while he pursues his graduate work in library and information sciences.

Emilio has earned a great reputation in his two years as a teacher's assistant. Although he is only three-quarters of the way through his library degree, the middle school principal, Lowell Markson, recommends him for the vacancy in the school library. Clothilde is the library media specialist at the Memorial Middle School in Plainview. Clothilde has worked there for five years and has been a school library media specialist for about seven years. She was a substitute for several years before securing the job at Memorial. Clothilde met Emilio when he came with some of his students to the library media center. She liked him personally but did not like the fact that he talked with some of the students in Spanish. Clothilde feels that unless the students are in bilingual Spanish classes, they should be spoken to and respond in English. This is an opinion that she does, however, keep to herself.

Clothilde has been alone in the school library media center since the retirement of Anthony Miller last year. There is a serious shortage of school library media specialists, and she has struggled with an uneven staffing pattern that included day-to-day substitutes, retired public librarians, and the like. She is not too happy with Emilio because he is not fully certified, but she has tremendous confidence in Lowell's judgment and decides not to prejudge Emilio.

Emilio feels grateful to Lowell for the chance to work full time as a school library media specialist. His salary is better than that of a teacher's assistant and so are the health-care benefits. With the additional salary he is able to take two courses a semester, leaving less than one year for completion of his MLS. Emilio is a very busy man.

Clothilde is single, and the library media center at Memorial is her whole life. She arrives early, stays late, and takes home professional reading, class preparation, and so on. She expects the same from Emilio. When Emilio arrives less than twenty minutes before the start of the school day and departs within thirty minutes of the close of the school day, she is not happy. When Emilio leaves the library media center during his lunch period, Clothilde becomes angry. She begins to think of him as lazy. In fact, Emilio is studying for his courses during lunchtime and needs quiet not found in the school library media center.

As the semester continues, Clothilde begins to keep a log of Emilio's comings and goings. She gives him tasks to complete for which he has no substantive background. He is not successful in completing them, and she documents this lack of success. By the time Christmas vacation rolls around, Clothilde has amassed quite a dossier of information about Emilio's petty shortcomings—days he forgot to back up the online catalog before going to lunch; times he let a student take out a book when the student already had one out that was overdue; days he spoke Spanish to Latino students in the library media center; days when he could not find a book on the shelf and Clothilde found it immediately. Clothilde's attitude is also showing in her daily dealings with Emilio. She constantly reminds him that she is "in charge," although she is not the supervisor. She belittles him in front of other staff members and one day told him that his emergency certificate was dependent upon her evaluation—something that is not true. Emilio has begun to talk with the union representative in his building about harassment on the job.

Questions

1. Is Clothilde harassing Emilio?
2. Clothilde is not the supervisor, and Emilio's certification is not dependent upon any evaluation from Clothilde. What makes her threaten him like this?
3. Is it any business of Clothilde's (or of any library media supervisor's) what an employee does on his or her lunchtime?
4. Should Clothilde have been involved in Lowell's decision to apply for an emergency certificate for Emilio?
5. What difference does it make if Emilio speaks Spanish to some of the students?
6. Is Emilio right to begin to speak to the union representative about his treatment by Clothilde?
7. Do emergency-certified school library media specialists have the same rights as fully certified ones? Who determines this?
8. Should Lowell step in and try to ameliorate this situation?

· 7 ·

Policies

FILTERS, FILTERS, FILTERS

It seemed almost too good to be true! Grady Nyamwange, the school library media specialist at Grant Avenue School, was delighted at the news that the board of education had approved his request for electronic media and Internet access for the library media center. When Blondi Mirrer, the principal of the Grant Avenue School, told him the good news the morning after the board meeting, Grady almost danced a little jig.

The allocation of money would provide for the installation of T-1 lines for the Internet, e-mail access, and also a number of online resources and CD-ROM products. Grady had a list of resources that he wanted, and he quickly made up a purchase order for them. He also asked for a CD-ROM tower that could be used for the master to network the computers in the library media center.

The installation of the necessary lines for Internet access had been planned a few years ago, but funds had never been available for the actual implementation. Now the time had come, and Grady was authorized to contact the phone and electrical companies to do the work.

A representative from the phone company came to the school and asked Grady to write up the request as a grant application, and that would qualify the school for special reduced rates. When Grady told Ms. Mirrer of the offer, she was delighted. It would make a good impression on the board members, she told Grady, and would make it possible for him to purchase more resources with the savings.

During the course of conversation with a fellow teacher in the lunchroom one day, Grady was asked about the methods he planned to use to protect his new resources. A few other teachers joined the discussion, and the topic of objectionable sites on the Internet came up. Grady admitted that he really had not thought much about that issue, but that it might be worth investigating. He filed it away in his mental notebook for a next-week project.

As work progressed on the installation of the resources, Grady began his research on the methods of protection in the use of the tools. He read some articles in journals and learned of various methods of blocking access to particular sites or types of sites. The articles were rather technical in content, so Grady went to the local electronics store to ask some questions. He was told that a number of products were on the market that could perform different types of functions. Blocking programs prevented users from accessing certain types of Web sites; some programs required the installer to specify the name of the site and then it would be blocked from use by library media center users.

Grady decided to bring the question about the type of blocking program to the next teachers' meeting and to ask the teachers what they thought should be blocked. The meeting turned into a very animated discussion, with teachers taking varied stances on what they felt was objectionable. When a list was finally compiled, Grady went to Blondi Mirrer to ask for clearance to purchase a rather comprehensive blocking program.

That issue settled, Grady was dismayed to hear a comment made by another teacher that perhaps firewalls were a better option for control. The firewalls were designed to block outsiders from entering the school library media center computers and destroying or corrupting the valuable electronic resources available on them or in the tower. So, Grady went to the computer store to inquire about firewalls. After listening to the salesperson's explanations, he placed an order for a firewall program.

Now, Grady thought, everything was just about set. The access lines were installed, and the Internet connection was hooked up on the computers. The tower was in place and the various CD-ROM programs were networked on each computer, complete with index table and use diagrams. It was time to let the students use the new programs. The library media center was abuzz with sounds of keyboarding and printers giving off sheets of text and graphics. Grady was so happy!

Questions

1. Are there any regulations about using blocking programs and firewalls?
2. Were Grady's reasons for using them valid?
3. What are the positions of the American Library Association (ALA) and the American Association of School Librarians (AASL) on the issue of blocking software?
4. Is the use of the blockers and firewalls a good educational practice? Are there any other alternatives?
5. Did Grady plan well for his new system? What should he have done?

MONEY, MONEY, MONEY—
JUST NOT ENOUGH, JUST NOT WHERE IT IS NEEDED

At the Dairylande School District, a large rural consolidated district composed of students from many farms and villages, the annual budget for the school library media center is $10 per child at the elementary level and $12 per child at the secondary level. This funding level was set about ten years ago. The money is for all print and nonprint materials, including subscriptions and reference works. Each year in October, an official census of the school is taken. That number is the one used when calculating the $10 or $12 per child. The funds are then allocated in early January, and all purchase decisions must be made before the end of April. Orders are generally delivered before the school year ends so that new materials are on hand when the fall semester begins.

Jon Quang is the newly hired library media supervisor for Dairylande. He has been a supervisor at other similar-sized districts and took the position at Dairylande because of its close proximity to a university with a highly regarded doctoral program in educational administration. Jon has no illusions about the challenges facing him with regard to funding. He begins by calling a meeting of all the library media specialists in the district. He asks them to bring statistics on how many students are enrolled according to the school census, how many books they expect to order with their allotment, as well as how many subscriptions, reference materials, and so on.

What Jon finds out is quite surprising. The school library media specialists at Dairylande have no funds to spend on the technology in their library media centers. The $10 a head is spent primarily on print items, with less than 20 percent set aside for CD products, online databases, and so on. The school library media specialists are forced to choose between supporting their traditional purchases of print items and supporting the technological needs of their expanding school library media centers. Unfortunately, regardless of the way the funds are allocated, each segment comes up short.

Jon must find a way to increase the funds currently allocated and create a new fund source for technology. Jon is a very resourceful person and begins to search the Internet, using a number of the meta-search engines like Dogpile and Mamma. What he finds are communities, not so very different from Dairylande, that have tackled this problem head on. They begin by linking the quality of instruction to the quality of the school library media center. From this connection, it is quite simple to devise a funding formula that meets the instructional needs for both traditional print and nonprint library resources, as well as support for the newer technologies.

Jon begins to prepare a presentation for the school board. This presentation will involve a selection of classroom teachers from across the district and some school library media specialists. Using Microsoft's PowerPoint software, they will "present" scenarios from the curricula at grades 4, 8, and 10—coincidentally, the grades at which state-mandated testing occurs. With these scenarios, they will demonstrate how the linking of print, nonprint, and technology resources in the school library media centers to the specific curricula will deteriorate with the present level of funding and what can be expected with increased dollars. Using his access to the Internet, Jon has created the following funding guidelines:

Maintenance of Hardware

- Determine the replacement rate by using 100 percent divided by the number of useful years of the product.
- Multiply the replacement rate by the total number of same items owned.
- Multiply this number by the average cost of the item.

Example: School library media specialist Lydia Ramos has fourteen IBM desktops on a high-speed line. The high-speed line was installed by the local phone company as a donation in kind, matching the grants from a regional foundation, which paid for the hardware. No maintenance costs are allocated. Each desktop cost approximately $1,000. Each machine includes: 350 MHz; 64 MB RAM; 100 MHz system bus; 6 GB hard drive; and Windows 98; and each is expected to last for five years. The replacement rate is thus calculated at: 100 percent divided by five, or 20 percent. To calculate the maintenance budget for fourteen machines would now be: 20 percent times fourteen machines times $1,000, or $2,800 per year.

Maintenance of Book Collection

The school library media center at one of the middle schools has 11,000 volumes on the shelf. With an average cost of $19 per book and the average life of a book equal to fifteen years, the maintenance budget would be as follows:

- Replacement rate: 100 percent divided by 15 years = 6.67 percent.
- Maintenance budget equals 6.67 percent times $19 per volume times 11,000 volumes or $14,003 per year to maintain the print collection.

Jon's presentation to the Dairylande School Board is well received. It is also widely covered by the news media. He has clearly done his homework.

Questions

1. What should Jon do now to get the funding formula changed?
2. What can he do to begin to institutionalize the recommendations for funding technology, print, and nonprint materials?
3. Is the formula that was presented realistic?
4. Does an Internet search yield more/better formulae for funding?
5. The formula presented in this case calls for a dramatic increase. Is there a way to phase in this increase?

6. If science books are included in formula, should their "shelf life" be shorter than fifteen years? How about for geography books?
7. Should the formula be modified to allow for a "shelf life" of print materials equal to ten years?

I THOUGHT THAT SHARING WAS A GOOD THING

Bob Budlong is the library media specialist at the West End Middle School. West End is a large, urban middle school with an enrollment of nearly 850 students in grades 6 through 8. Bob has been the library media specialist there for nearly six years. He is an active person and gives the job his great energy and his best work. For relaxation, Bob writes. He started off writing a column for the local newspaper that talked about books that students should read. From there, he moved on to reviewing titles for the newspaper and eventually for *School Library Journal* and other review media. Lately, Bob has been writing short stories and poetry. He feels that this is the way that he can express himself and find his inner soul.

The principal at West End, Wayne Cruz, is a friend of Bob's and they often socialize with one another's families. Both men arrived at West End at around the same time and have a great deal in common—high energy, commitment to the students, and an easygoing manner. Both men are also risk takers—they will try a new program or product if they believe it will help their students.

Recently, Wayne became discouraged over the lack of state and local funding for innovative products and projects focused around technology. He shares his frustration with Bob, who suggests that grant writing might just close the gap between student and teacher needs and local and state funding. Wayne encourages Bob, who seems to have a knack for writing. With his typical enthusiastic bent, Bob identifies local foundations and organizations that provide funds for literacy and technology. He does an Internet search using Dogpile.com to identify regional and national sources that provide similar funds. He talks with colleagues on various listservs about sources they have used.

Policies

Eventually, Bob begins to ask for and receive RFPs (Request for Proposal) from several funding agencies that look like they might be appropriate. Each funding source RFP has its own format, but most want a brief description of the project, a budget, and some indication of accountability and sustainability, as well as the right to publicize the project. Bob tackles only RFPs that provide funding for technology and literary projects. He wants to get his feet wet in this very narrow niche of the funding world. Once he develops his expertise, then he would like to branch out in broader arenas. When Bob writes, he tackles the RFP as if it were his column. He begins by stating what he needs and how he will use it in terms of a scenario. Once this is complete, he works with Wayne on the budget part and with the central office staff on the public relations pieces. He makes sure that each project is unique and only makes one funding request for that project. He knows that he should now develop a project and then blanket the funding world with requests on behalf of the project. What would he do if there were three or four agencies that wanted to fund the same project?

Bob sends off several somewhat related requests to different funding agencies. He receives, in short order, money for two of the four projects that he wants to initiate. The first project requires $12,000 to set up a program for reluctant readers. Using Scholastic's Read 180 Program, this project links numerous pieces of middle-school literature to an innovative reading program developed at Vanderbilt University. Students read in large groups, small groups, and individually; they use books on tape and in print format. Their progress is monitored using the already existing Windows NT lab and is staffed by the reading specialist already on duty. The software is proprietary and specially designed to run in an NT environment.

The second project for which Bob receives funding is to supplement the reading from the Scholastic Read 180 Program by adding a periodical component. Bob uses the $5,000 for this project to purchase numerous periodicals in hard copy and to subscribe to several indexes in CD-ROM format. Most of the indexes come from the H. W. Wilson Company and include *Biography Index* (updated quarterly on CD-ROM), *Current Biography* (updated annually on CD-ROM), and *The Reader's Guide for Young People* (updated monthly on CD-ROM). All are purchased with the idea that they will run on only one station, so Bob sets up his Internet search stations to each accommodate one of these products. Linking these two projects is a stroke of genius—students can read about an event or people in the Scholastic Read 180 Program and then do "real" research about the event, using one of the CD-ROM products. Wayne is ecstatic and is sure that these two programs combined will enhance student achievement. Bob is thrilled that his initial grant-writing efforts are so successful, and he begins to write for more products and services—no longer limiting himself to such a narrow range. He continues to be successful.

At the end of the second year of his program for the H. W. Wilson indexes, Bob has about fifteen CD-ROMs from the *Reader's Guide for Young People,* at least two for *Current Biography,* and a half-dozen for *Biography Index*. He really doesn't want to use the older ones, as they do not contain the most current information. He keeps the back CD-ROMs in his office but often thinks about sharing them with his colleagues. At one of the monthly library media specialist meetings, Bob talks about search strategies using the Wilson Indexes. When he indicates that he has back files on CD-ROM, his colleagues clamor for him to share the older ones with them. He begins to question why he is keeping them in his office and sends off the *Current Biography, Reader's Guide for Young People,* and *Biography Index* CD-ROMs to some of the other middle- and high-school libraries. Bob doesn't think that he is violating any sort of laws by just sharing them within the district. After all, he really isn't cutting into the profits of the H. W. Wilson Company since the schools he is sending the older products to don't have the money to subscribe anyway. Besides which, he is still keeping the products in the district.

Questions

1. Should Bob be doing this?
2. What does H. W. Wilson say about its older CD-ROMs?
3. Is Bob jeopardizing future grants by engaging in this sharing of CD products?
4. Are the CD police going to swoop down on West End Middle School and charge Bob with copyright violation?

5. If there is a legal violation, is Bob liable? How about Wayne? The fund source? The district?

GET THAT FILTHY BOOK OUT OF HERE!

Mark Fuentes is the library media specialist at the Mount Grey Junior High School. He is a hard worker and truly committed to his school and his students. He is active in his state association and currently serves as its representative to the statewide children's book award committee. In that capacity, Mark gets lots of free publications. Since he is serving a three-year term, the publishers know about his work on the committee and see to it that any and all potential nominees for the book award are sent to him. Mark holds on to all of the books that he receives until the fifteen official nominees are known. Then, if the book is age- and interest-appropriate for the collection at Mount Grey, he adds it in. Otherwise, he sends the title along to one of the other sites in the district. Mark does not read every book he adds to the collection at Mount Grey—he couldn't possibly keep up. Instead, he relies on book reviews, author and publisher reputation, and recommendations from colleagues across the state. The state association has an active listserv where new titles often are discussed and recommendations are made prior to their inclusion in one of the standard review media.

Late one Thursday afternoon, Mark is sitting at his desk reading the incoming mail and checking in some periodicals. The phone rings and a woman asks for him by name. She identifies herself—Rachel Duarte—and says she is the parent of a seventh-grader. Now, Mark often receives calls from parents—in fact, he encourages parents to call the library media center and includes the phone number on any correspondence that goes out. Furthermore, he serves as treasurer of the PTO and has lots of conversations with parents about everything under the sun—not just library media center–related items. As the parent begins to speak, Mark tunes in closely to what she is saying. She is very unhappy about a book that her son Brandon has brought home.

Brandon is a seventh-grader and a rather high-spirited young man. Brandon is also an excellent reader and is often in the library media center. Brandon's English teacher is very involved in the New Standards Program. He is certain that this will ensure success for all of his students. The NCEE (National Center on Education and the Economy) recommends that each middle grade or junior high school student read at least twenty-five books per year. To that end, Brandon's teacher expects a written book report every two weeks during the school year. The English teacher, Mr. Arturo, works closely with Mark to identify titles and genres that they think will appeal to the students. They have been doing this for the last few years and have had good success. In the eighth-grade writing assessment and the language arts tests, Mr. Arturo's students scored among the highest at Mount Grey. Since Mount Grey loops students for seventh and eighth grade, Mr. Arturo is back again teaching seventh grade. The book report that is due in two weeks offers students a choice—any fiction title as long as animals play a key role in the story. In some of the stories animals are the main characters, while in others, the animal and its plight play a central role in the development of the plot. Mark and Mr. Arturo select about 100 titles from the Mount Grey collection. The works span a variety of reading and interest levels, but all are at least 100 pages. The books are placed on a large cart, and a sign is posted, indicating that they are for Mr. Arturo's seventh-grade English classes.

During a two-day period, all of Mr. Arturo's students come to the library media center to select a book—Brandon Duarte is one of them. Brandon checks out his book and takes it home that afternoon. An eager reader, he begins to read it on the bus and continues at his house. About thirty minutes into reading the book, Brandon goes out to the kitchen and reads part of the book to his mother. He does this, he tells her, because the "book has lots of swears in it." At this, his mother takes the book and calls Mark Fuentes at school to lodge her complaint.

Mark has read lots of things over his professional career about intellectual freedom challenges and he supports the concept of intellectual freedom. Mark, however, is a very cautious individual. He is very careful in selecting and adding items to his collection—he does not want to become a "poster boy" for the American Library Association Intellectual Freedom Committee. Mrs. Duarte identifies Brandon's book as *Dog Eat Dog* by Chris Lynch. While Mrs. Duarte is speaking, Mark is feeling sick to his stomach—How could this be happening to him? Where is this situation going? Isn't this book part of a trilogy and doesn't Mount Grey own all three? Mrs. Duarte is very polite on the phone, but she is also very determined. When Mark tells her that the book has been well reviewed and is recommended for reluctant readers, she tells him that she feels he will do nothing about her concern and so she plans on contacting the superintendent. She wants the book withdrawn from the collection. Mark tells her that, of course, she is free to contact the superintendent but that she should read the book in its entirety. She says she will not read such filth and may even throw it out. Mark is horrified and informs her that the book is checked out to her son and if it is not returned, he is financially liable. The conversation ends on a polite but cold note, and Mark leaves for home, wondering what tomorrow will bring.

Mark sleeps poorly that night and the next morning is in the library media center earlier than normal. As expected, the principal stops in and asks him what is he doing "buying dirty books"? The principal is joking, but Mark still feels sick in the bottom of his stomach. He is uncomfortable with the banter that the principal wishes to engage in. Later that day, Mark is asked to come to the office of the assistant superintendent for teaching and learning. Mr. Woodrow wishes to speak with him about a parent concern. When Mark gets to the assistant superintendent's office, Mr. Woodrow asks him if it is true that he told Mrs. Duarte that should her son not return the book, he would be financially liable? Mark confirms this, and Mr. Woodrow starts to laugh. "That really caught her off-guard," he said. "She looked at the dust jacket and found out how much she would have to pay, so she stopped by this morning and dropped off the book. She does not want it to go back on the shelf, and I told her I would look into it." Mark is relieved. Mr. Woodrow has a reputation for fairness and for being a reflective thinker.

Mr. Woodrow asks Mark to get him the latest reviews and any other information about the book and the author. He promises Mark that he will read the book from cover to cover and then make his decision. Mark goes home feeling much better. The next morning he calls the publisher and gets the book's editor on the phone. She faxes him lots of reviews and offers to call the assistant superintendent and discuss the book with him. Mark tells her he will hold off on any direct contact, but he appreciates the offer. He gets the reviews off to Mr. Woodrow in a timely manner and waits to hear an answer.

The book is eventually returned to Mark, and he receives a handwritten note from Mr. Woodrow. The book is to be kept at the Mount Grey Library Media Center, but Mark is not to call too much attention to it. The mother's objections to the subject matter and the language—dog fighting and profanity—are ignored. In fact, Mr. Woodrow does not follow up with the mother and tells Mark that she probably has forgotten all about it. Mark puts the book on the shelf, vowing never to include it in any book talks, book exhibits, or reading lists.

Questions

1. Where is the reconsideration form and policy in this situation? Is there one? Should there be one?
2. If there is one, should it include allowing the assistant superintendent for teaching and learning the ability to make the decision about the book's fate?
3. What could/should Mark have done differently when contacted by Mrs. Duarte?
4. Should Mark have notified his colleagues via their very active listserv about this challenge?
5. Is the assistant superintendent correct in suggesting to Mark that he put the book back on the shelf but not call attention to it?
6. Is it likely that Mrs. Duarte will just go away and let this issue die?
7. Should Mark have contacted his local professional association or ALA when this challenge was first received?
8. Should Mark have allowed/encouraged the publisher to get directly involved in this incident and speak to the assistant superintendent?

I DIDN'T BORROW THE BOOKS FROM THE PUBLIC LIBRARY, SO WHY SHOULD I WORRY IF THEY ARE MISSING?

Pascal DeTours is the school library media specialist at the Greenaway Elementary School. Prior to coming to Greenaway, he worked at the municipal library. His responsibilities there included interlibrary loan, circulation, and finally the children's room. Pascal went part time to college and then on to library school. His work at the public library gave him great respect for classroom teachers and for school library media specialists. He was anxious to join their ranks, so when a position opened up at Greenaway he quickly applied.

Pascal had a great reputation at the municipal library among teachers, other librarians, and students. He was fortunate to be selected as the library media specialist at Greenaway and set about creating the same type of working environment there that he had at the municipal library. Pascal feels that his roles of teacher, instructional partner, information specialist, and program administrator allow him to fill a unique niche in helping the entire school community to function intelligently in the Information Age. On a daily basis, Pascal lives and breathes the ideal of Information Power. By providing access above and beyond his collection, Pascal ensures that the school community at Greenaway Elementary effectively uses ideas and information.

Although Pascal lives and breathes the ideals, he is faced with the reality of an aging collection, insufficient funding, a fixed schedule of classes, and limited technology. He does have Internet access in the library media center and enough workstations for approximately one-half of the students in a classroom to search at the same time. He also has an online catalog but only two search stations. He is attempting to secure funding to update the online catalog so that all of the Internet stations will also function as search stations for the online catalog. Pascal finds himself caught financially between the demands of print and electronic resources. He also had to balance the need for new chairs and tables with the need for new hardware.

One of the most successful ways Pascal has found to balance the demands on his print collection with the demand for electronic sources is to maximize his use of the collection at the municipal library. Since he worked there for so many years, he is intimately familiar with the collection. He knows that the municipal library offers teachers what they call a "classroom card." This allows a teacher to borrow up to fifty items at one time. The books have a loan period of sixty days, and if materials are returned late, there is no fine. Each card is the responsibility of the individual teacher, although the principal of the school must countersign the application for the "classroom card." Pascal strongly encourages the teachers at Greenaway to take advantage of this card.

Beatrice Connor-Meserve is a twenty-year veteran of the Greenaway Elementary School. She has taught fifth grade for most of her years at Greenaway. She does lots of writing across the curriculum and does teach around several large themes each year. Unfortunately, the themes never change and she often appears bored with the projects. Students are fearful of her wrath and do not want to be assigned to her classroom. She points with pride each quarter, however, when the middle-school honor roll is published in the paper. More students from her fifth grade are successful in sixth grade than from any other fifth grade in the district.

Beatrice is preparing her annual Egypt unit. She wants the students to select research topics from among a select list. Each student must have a written research report with footnotes and a bibliography. Beatrice notifies Pascal that she would like him to assist her students when they come to the library media center each week. She wants each student to narrow down the topic he or she has chosen and begin to select appropriate print resources. She has a form for footnotes and bibliography, which she shares with Pascal. By the end of the first class on this assignment, it is clear to Pascal that he cannot begin to support the information needs of these students. He talks with Beatrice at lunch and asks her about getting and using a "classroom card" at the municipal library. She tells him that she does not have time to go there, and it is too much trouble to drag all the books back to her classroom. She tells him that she will encourage the children to go to the municipal library themselves.

Pascal knows full well that the students are not likely to get to the municipal library themselves. He has a "classroom card" that he decides to use for Beatrice's project. Pascal borrows about forty titles on the range of topics that the children are permitted to select from. He creates abbreviated MARC records in his online catalog for these books and checks them out to the children. It is a real pain to do this, but he believes that the ideals of Information Power support his efforts in this area. Beatrice is very impressed with the materials that Pascal has secured and asks to borrow some for use in her classroom. Pascal checks about eight of them out to her. As the children complete work on their projects, the books borrowed from the municipal library are returned to Pascal, who in turn returns them to the municipal library. About four weeks after the assignment has ended, Pascal is at the municipal library when a former colleague mentions that he still has five books out on ancient Egypt. Pascal assures her that he will check his records at the school and take care of things.

Upon checking the online catalog, Pascal finds that the missing five books are checked out to none other than Beatrice Connor-Meserve. He sends her a note and, after two or three days, seeks her out before school one morning. Beatrice claims that she does not have the books and that she returned them when the project ended. Pascal is doubtful, as the classroom is quite a mess and he is not sure she could find anything. He waits for several weeks, keeping his eyes open for strange books in the book return. At the end of another month he again speaks with Beatrice about the missing books. She tells him that, to the best of her knowledge, the books were returned. They were not checked out to her from the municipal library and the problem is not hers. She refuses to discuss the matter further.

Questions

1. Should Pascal force the issue with Beatrice by involving the principal?
2. Since the books were checked out to Pascal, isn't he the responsible party?
3. Is it ethical to check out books that rightfully belong to the municipal library through the school library media center's online catalog?
4. Is this some type of interlibrary loan issue?

5. What should Pascal do about this problem now? How can it be avoided in the future?
6. Should the municipal library have a policy about lost books? What should it include?

I AM SURE THAT I PAID FOR THAT

The City of Plaintown has a rigid policy with regard to purchases of any items for use by the city or its agencies. All requests must be accompanied by a PR (Purchase Requisition) and forwarded with appropriate budget codes and signatures to the Purchasing Office. The purpose behind this process is to guarantee that all funds are spent wisely, that bidding procedures are followed correctly, and that the City of Plaintown gets the most for its money. The policy extends to the Plaintown School Department, which organizationally is considered one of the city's agencies. Although the purchase of materials is quite structured, the system moves rapidly to issue POs (Purchase Orders). These are the legally binding documents that formalize a relationship between the City of Plaintown and the vendor. No purchases are to be made without following the route of PR to PO. Once the PO is issued, the vendor has thirty days to ship the requested item and the city then has an additional thirty days after receipt to pay for the item. The city has an AAA+ rating for its financial transactions, and all employees are made aware of the city's fiscal policies and procedures.

Marta Amaral is the library media specialist at the Western Avenue Elementary School in Plaintown. Marta has been a teacher in Plaintown for several years and recently completed her graduate work in library science. She accepted the position at Western Avenue this past September and eagerly tackled her work there. She weeded the collection, developed a reading program using senior citizens from the neighborhood to read to the students in the lower grades, and published reading lists for all of the grades in the building. She is actively soliciting grant money to build the collection and to install an online catalog. As a classroom teacher, Marta had no opportunity to purchase books in the assorted elementary schools where she worked. Each spring she advised her principal what textbooks she needed to have replaced for the upcoming year. Her consumable supplies (pencils, writing paper, glue, crayons, and the like) were ordered directly by the stock clerk at the building. All purchases followed the protocol for purchases laid down by the City, but Marta was not even aware of this protocol; she simply submitted requests in memo form to her principal and when school opened in September, the items were in the building.

When Marta transferred to the school library media center at Western Avenue, she attended the orientation for new school library media specialists. She learned there about the time line for book orders, the requirements for processing, and ways to create an inviting, print-rich library media center. The library media supervisors tell Marta that each month the school library media specialists meet informally to share concerns and ideas and that Marta will be added to the listserv maintained by the supervisor to keep folks up-to-date with emerging issues. Marta eagerly undertakes her new responsibilities, attends the monthly meetings, and thoroughly enjoys her work.

In April Marta receives a call from the New Media Publishing Group. The telemarketer talks with Marta at length about New Media's product line of award-winning books for elementary schools. Marta listens eagerly and is enthusiastic about the call. She tells the telemarketer that she would love to preview their current product line and authorizes the shipment of three cartons (approximately seventy-five titles) to the Library Media Center at Western Avenue Elementary School. The cartons arrive the next week and Marta signs the delivery slip. She loves the books and wants to buy them. She tells her principal that she needs $987.00 from his budget to purchase these wonderful, age- and interest-appropriate titles. The principal tells her that he has some discretionary money and that he will also talk with the PTO president. He is sure that the seventy-five books can be paid for from these funds.

The next day, Marta falls in her kitchen, breaks her ankle in three places, and remains home on sick leave for the remainder of the school year. A substitute teacher is sent to work in the school library media center. When the new term arrives in September, Marta accepts a transfer to the Field Street Middle School. She and her husband return one afternoon to clear out her personal possessions from

Western Avenue. The new school library media specialist is Hector Morales. Hector is a recent graduate of the Library School, and this is his first job. He has never been a classroom teacher and hopes that his enthusiasm will make up for his lack of experience. He finds the book order in cartons in the room and shelves all of the books. He files whatever cards he finds and creates shelflist cards for those books without a full set of catalog cards. He keeps a record of these so that he can eventually order card sets. His classroom management skills are good, and the teachers and students are pleased that he has joined the faculty at Western Avenue.

Notices arrive in the mail almost weekly from New Media Publishing Group. They are initially reminders and then the tone becomes more demanding. Hector returns the notices to the principal, who ignores them. He feels that this is just time-delayed paperwork. After two months, phone calls come to the school for Marta Amaral. Upon being told by the school secretary that Marta does not work at Western Avenue any longer, the caller asks to be put through to the school library media center. Hector identifies himself at the school library media center but disavows all knowledge of the situation of the unpaid and now missing titles. Soon, notices of nonpayment arrive but now addressed to Hector. He calls the library media supervisor and asks for her help. She in turn contacts Marta at Field Street Middle School. Marta at first says that she knows nothing about this; then she claims that the PTO paid for the materials. Finally, she says that it was her plan to have the city pay for the materials by generating a PR and then notifying the company that when they received the PO, not to ship, as Marta already had the books on hand. Since no one can even find the books at Western Avenue, the supervisor is unsure of how to proceed. Meanwhile, New Media Publishing Group is threatening to turn the matter over to a collection agency.

Questions

1. Marta has clearly lied about the handling of the matter. What course of action should the library media supervisor initiate? Did Marta break any laws?
2. Who is responsible for the books? Marta? The principal? Are both people agents of the City of Plaintown?

3. Should the library media supervisor have warned Marta and the other school library media specialists about accepting preview collections?
4. Should the telemarketers know about the city's purchasing procedures? How? Why?

SELLING TO CHILDREN—RIGHT, WRONG, LEGAL?

Each year at the Messenger Elementary School, the school library media specialist holds two extremely successful book fairs. Bopha Yer, the library media specialist at Messenger, is a legend among her colleagues. She holds her first book fair of the academic year in late September, with the PTO-sponsored open house. The second book fair is usually held during the last full week of May. This one is focused around the reading list that Bopha has created for the summer. Bopha has held her very successful book fairs since she came to Messenger nine years ago.

The money from the book fairs makes a serious contribution to the operation of the school library media center. Initially, the money was about $1,500 per year. Each year, that sum creeps up. Recently, Bopha's book fairs returned a profit of $3,000 to the coffers of the Messenger Elementary School Library Media Center. Bopha has been consistent in using the same book fair company at Messenger. Its sales reps are happy to have her business and each year offer her an incentive to continue to book with them. The Triumph Book Fair Company is an offshoot of the Triumph Publishing Company. Its books are high quality and many are award winners. It has diverse product lines that feature picture books, adult trade books, cookbooks, and, of course, chapter reading books that are age- and interest-appropriate for elementary grades.

The company offers several profit plans—some allow the school to take between 30 and 50 percent of the gross receipts, some allow for all profits to be taken in merchandise, and others allow a combination. Bopha always takes the percentage of the gross receipts. She is a high-volume customer of Triumph and often winds up taking 40 percent of the gross receipts as her profit, with the balance returning to Triumph along with the unsold books. Each year Triumph hosts a luncheon for new and returning customers to preview its new line. At the end of the luncheon, there are numerous gifts of pens, pencils, bags, posters, and paperback books. Sometimes, an author from Triumph will speak at the luncheon, and the attendees receive autographed copies of the speaker's books. Bopha takes all of these treasures and keeps them until it is time for the book fair. In addition, Bopha is sure to pick up tablets, pencils, and pens at any conferences she attends. All of these she holds aside until her book fair, whether in September or May.

The Triumph Book Fair is set up at the school the week of the September open house. This year, Bopha, as usual, does not unpack any of the posters, pencils, or markers from the company. She has her own supply of these, which she sells to the children. These are generally ones that Bopha has picked up at the Triumph luncheon or that she has received from various publishers as incentives. Bopha also purchases inexpensive items like markers and stickers at the local office supply warehouse. These she sells to the children, as well as the autographed copies of special books she received at the Triumph luncheon. The markers and stickers Bopha generally buys at the rate of ten per dollar. She sells them to the children at twenty-five cents each, creating a profit of fifteen cents per item. At the end of the week, Bopha has cleared $1,712 from the book fair. About $300 of that is money generated by the sale of small things such as stickers and pencils, which Bopha puts out along with the items from the Triumph Book Fair Company.

Bopha keeps about $100 of the profit as seed money for the book fair she will hold in the spring. She deposits the rest of the money into the school checking account. This money will be used to purchase some printer cartridges, a new series of books on the planets, and the complete set of the Dear America series. The district has a stringent accounting procedure for the school checkbook, and Bopha is careful to follow it.

Bopha feels that her book fairs are so successful because each child, no matter how much or how little money he or she has to spend, can make a purchase. She is generous to a fault with the children. Often a child will be considerably short of the necessary funds to buy a particular item. Bopha takes what the child has and allows the purchase, cutting her own profit to supply the wanted item. She keeps meticulous track of "her money" and the money belonging to Triumph. She tags all of the non-Triumph items with a color code and is quickly able to determine which items generated what profit.

As is the custom with a book fair, Bopha completes the accounting sheet for Triumph, returns its share of the gross income, and deposits the rest into the school checking account. She does not tell Triumph, or anyone for that matter, that she sells items herself at the Triumph Book Fair. Her principal knows that she keeps about $100 from each book fair for the start-up of the next fair.

Questions

1. Is it legal to sell things during the book fair that are not supplied by the company?
2. How does Bopha select the company and the specific profit plan?
3. Does she/should she have input from teachers, administration, and so on?
4. Should there be a district-wide policy on book fairs, especially one that addresses selling supplementary items as Bopha does?

· 8 ·

Personnel

MANAGING FROM AFAR, OR BUTTING IN WHERE YOU DON'T BELONG?

Michael Johnson is a certified school library media specialist who lives in Lake City. Lake City is the county seat for the county of Lakeville, and Michael is well known in the local area. He has been living and working there for his entire professional career. He went to high school in Lake City and was quite the athlete. His two children followed in his footsteps. Michael has served on the board of the United Way and several other community agencies. His demeanor and sense of community have earned him wide respect.

Michael is at a basketball game at the high school one evening when he sits next to Greg Moore, one of the elementary principals. After the usual amenities, Greg tells Michael that he is having a problem. Specifically, he wants Michael to advise him on a deteriorating situation in the school library media center at Foster Elementary School. As Greg explains, the school library media specialist there is just a flake (although a tenured one), and the library is very disorganized, perhaps even worse. The library media specialist is often absent; she sometimes leaves at lunch and doesn't return. Furthermore, Greg explains, the teachers have lost all respect for her. The library media center is grossly underutilized, and teachers are reluctant to send their classes for any of the research or open library times found in the library media specialist's schedule.

Michael listens sympathetically. He has known Greg for many years and although he has never worked for him, he knows that he consistently supports the library media center at Foster Elementary.

Furthermore, he knows that Greg demands a great deal from teachers and staff assigned there, but that is no more than Greg demands from himself. The basketball game continues, and Greg and Michael agree to meet at another date. Michael is based at Meadow Elementary, another elementary school in the district. His school is fully automated, just like Foster Elementary.

About a week after the basketball game, a phone call from Greg comes in. Michael talks with Greg for about half an hour. He tells Greg that he should look at the online catalog and ask the library media specialist to print from the system a record of how much circulation has occurred this month. He then tells Greg that he should request these data at the beginning of each month so that he can begin to build a basis for comparison. Next, Michael tells Greg that the library media specialist should be keeping a log of her classes—both those that come on a fixed schedule and those that come in when there is open library or research time. Michael tells Greg that this would give him an idea of how effectively the library media specialist at Foster is using her time.

Greg thinks that Michael's ideas are good ones and sends a written memo to the library media specialist, asking her to provide him with this type of monthly information. She complains to the library media supervisor that the principal is harassing her. There is a brief meeting, with no resolution of the issue. Greg drops the matter for the time being, and things go along as they have. About two months later, Greg calls Michael and asks for a face-to-face meeting. He wants to discuss further strategies for dealing with the inept library media specialist at Foster. Michael agrees to the meeting but asks that Greg come to Meadow Elementary. At this meeting, Greg asks Michael to "walk him through" a typical day in the life of a school library media specialist—one with a combination of a fixed and flexible schedule in an elementary school. Michael does this and Greg takes copious notes.

At the end of their meeting, Greg tells Michael that he has a whole new game plan for dealing with the Foster Elementary School library media specialist. He tells Michael that he is going to bury her with paperwork—one report after another until she either quits or moves to another school. He also plans to pop in on her on a regular basis to see that the reports she will be required to submit are connected to the reality of the library media center's functioning.

Michael is not particularly encouraged at this route, but since it is really not his concern, he voices no opinion.

The next week, Michael is shocked to receive a call from the school library media supervisor. She tells Michael that the library media specialist at Foster has filed a grievance against Greg for harassment. Furthermore, the grievance alleges that Michael is helping Greg to harass her by providing comparative data between Foster and Meadow. In other words, Michael is helping Greg to set the woman up. The library media supervisor suggests that Michael might want to discuss this matter privately with the bargaining unit and he might wish to engage private counsel. She confides to Michael that he has stepped into her domain and that she herself is considering disciplinary action against him. Michael goes home extremely distraught. How on earth did he get himself into the middle of this?

Questions

1. Did Greg step over the bounds of propriety in his discussion with Michael?
2. Should Michael have spoken so freely with Greg at the basketball game?
3. Did Michael behave inappropriately in allowing Greg to see how his facility operated on a daily basis?
4. What is the role of the school library media supervisor in the case of a school library media specialist such as the one found at Foster?
5. What could/should Greg have done as a first step to improve the quality of library media service at Foster?
6. What is the role of colleagues within a bargaining unit? Are Michael and the school library media specialist at Foster equal, or is one more equal than the other?
7. Is there a liability issue for Michael?

LET THEM LEARN ALPHABETICAL ORDER

Pine Middle School is located in the affluent suburban town of Pine Manor. The students are a homogeneous group of fifth- through eighth-graders. Most of the students walk to school and those who are bused are still drawn from the same affluent area. There are neither ESL students at Pine Middle School nor a free lunch program. The number of minority children is less than 10 percent, out of an enrollment of 800. The minority children are primarily African-American or Japanese. Both minority groups are children of employees of the nearby university.

Juanita Gomez is the library media specialist at Pine Middle School. Juanita resides in Pine Manor, and her husband is the head of pediatrics at the university medical school. Juanita is the mother of three children, all of whom attended Pine Middle School. Now, they are in graduate school or working, and Juanita returned full time to the workplace about six years ago when her youngest daughter left for college.

Juanita graduated from college and library school in the early 1970s. She married immediately upon graduation and stayed at home for over twenty years. She is an avid reader, does beautiful needlepoint, and enjoys traveling to New York to see the museum collections and Broadway shows. Juanita returned to work because she felt that she had something to offer to the students in Pine Manor. She initially worked in the local elementary school but always loved the middle grades. Thus, when the position of school library media specialist opened up at Pine Middle School, she jumped at the chance to transfer.

Pine Middle School has everything a school library media center could possibly want or need. The large physical plant has a functional yet attractive layout. There is a full-time clerk plus a bevy of parent volunteers. The collection is up-to-date and the funding is well above the state standards for middle school. Recently, the school has adopted the NCEE standards. Juanita is well aware of the English/language arts requirement that each student read twenty-five or more books across several genres. Accordingly, the budget has been increased to allow for this new initiative, and Juanita has spent considerable time adding to the titles suggested by the NCEE.

Pine Middle School was the first in the state to be completely automated. The library media center boasts two circulation stations, a server, and one search station. There is a high-speed line with fifteen multimedia stations. Both CD-ROMs and the Internet can be used at any of these fifteen. The library media center operates on a flexible schedule and is very busy. Juanita goes above and beyond for the students and staff in supplying access and instruction.

The nearby university has a large education department and a library school. Although Juanita has often thought about it, she has never taken a student teacher in the library media center. This year, she decides that it would be a great way to get more involved in her profession. Besides, she has such a great operation at Pine Middle School; it will give an entry-level library media specialist something to aspire to. She contacts Dr. Michael Chase and tells him that she would be able to take a student teacher in the spring. Dr. Chase is thrilled. He is aware of the reputation that Pine Middle has among other middle schools in the region. He knows just the person to place with Juanita.

In early December, Juanita receives a call from the library school student who has been assigned as Juanita's student teacher. Sara Levy is a former classroom teacher who took about ten years off to raise her family. She returned to the workforce about two years ago and was placed as a substitute in the school library media center. Sara loved the work and decided to pursue a certificate as a school library media specialist. She has never met Juanita but has heard a great deal about the great school library media center at Pine Middle School.

Juanita invites Sara to come to Pine Middle School the following week. She wants to review their mutual expectations for the student teaching. Juanita also feels that this will give her a chance to get to know a little about Sara in a more relaxed atmosphere. The date is set and Sara meets Juanita, who gives her the tour of the school library media center; introduces her to faculty, staff, and administration; and lays out what she expects from Sara. Sara is impressed with the facility and the friendliness of the staff. There is a real positive feeling among the staff members for Juanita and her efforts. As their time together ends, Sara comments on the lack of more than one search station for the online catalog. She notices a card catalog in the center of the reference area and students continuously using it. She inquires why it is still there, much less being used. Sara goes on further to inquire about the time and cost of maintaining such a dinosaur in an increasingly technologically rich environment.

Juanita has heard these statements before. She explains to Sara that middle-school children need practice with alphabetical order. The best way to get this practice is to maintain the card catalog. That way, the children search alphabetically for the books by author, title, and subject. Thus, their spelling and alphabetical-order skills are reinforced on a continual basis. This, Juanita explains, is really what authentic assessment is all about. Sara pursues the matter by inquiring about the single search station. Sara tells her that it is used exclusively by the adults in the school. The clerk files all cards in the card catalog and maintains a paper shelflist. The shelflist is used as a back-up in case the server fails. Sara is not experienced enough to counter any of the claims that Juanita has made, but she has an uneasy feeling about her approaching student-teaching experience.

Questions

1. Is maintaining a card catalog in a technologically sophisticated school library media center a cost-effective option?
2. What is the real cost of maintaining the card catalog and paper shelflist?
3. Is forcing students to use the card catalog really authentic assessment? Is it teaching them alphabetical order and spelling skills?
4. What should Sara do about this situation? Do you think Dr. Chase is aware of this?
5. Should Dr. Chase have visited Pine Middle School before he placed Sara Levy there as a student teacher?

WHO PAYS FOR PROFESSIONAL DEVELOPMENT?

The State School Library Association holds its annual conference each spring. It is a full-day affair with over 400 school library media specialists in attendance. It is a time to meet old friends, make new ones, and catch up on the latest happenings in the world of the school library media specialist. The conference committee plans all year to bring a balanced program—print and electronic products, speakers, and presentations—to its membership. The organization has a hefty checking and savings account balance, so speaker fees are not really a problem. The cost for registration generally covers the actual conference expenses, exclusive of these fees. Sometimes the association is able to combine its conference with an author's speaking tour to minimize travel expenses. All in all, the event is well planned and well attended, and the evaluations of the programs are excellent.

Carol Danoff has been a member of the State School Library Association since receiving her MLS in 1981. She has been active in the association, writing a column for the newsletter, hosting programs, and working on the conference committee. Carol's work on the conference committee has made her question the cost of the annual conference. Each year, the association dips into its savings accounts to cover the cost of the speakers. The registrations pay for printing, food, the conference site, and so on, but Carol feels that unless the conference is run on a pay-as-you-go basis, the association will eventually run out of funds.

Well respected in her field, Carol Danoff is selected as the chair of this year's conference committee. She decides that the committee should consider increasing the cost of registration. This move would force the association to look critically at fiscal management and to begin to cover all costs associated with the conference with the registration fee. Carol Danoff is successful in her efforts to increase the registration fee. In due course the program is printed, and the conference registrations start coming in. There are some grumblings about the cost, but registrations seem unaffected.

On the day of the conference, Carol is manning the registration desk. The conference is sold out, and there are several walk-ins. The first walk-in is Mickey, an elementary school library media specialist. Mickey is rude at the registration desk and demands admission. Carol tells her that there is no room—lunch is sold out and there are no seats for the keynote address. Without a badge, the exhibits and general sessions will be closed to Mickey. Mickey is furious but decides that since she has already requested the professional leave, she will just go home and catch up on her housework. Carol cautions Mickey that since she is being denied admission to the conference, she should return to her school for the day. Mickey just says she will take care of things. Carol is troubled, as they are both in the same district and the superintendent always checks on leaves for the State Association Conference.

The second incident also involves school library media specialists from Carol's district. Charlie and Jim are both middle school library media specialists who generally meet at the registration desk at the conference to catch up on things. Both grumble, good-naturedly, about the increased cost of registration. Charlie tells Jim that he doesn't care about the cost, as his principal has paid the registration. Jim applied to his school's Professional Development Committee for payment of the cost of the conference, but it was denied. Jim asks how Charlie's registration came to be paid while his own was denied.

Charlie tells Jim that the principal set aside money for ongoing Professional Development throughout the year. Each teacher applies for the money he or she needs, and the Professional Development Committee reviews the application and provides funding based upon merit. Charlie tells Jim that he has been reading about the concept of Individual Professional Development Plans and has crafted one for himself. He then selects conferences and courses in line with his plan. So far, the school has paid for the State Association conference and a three-credit graduate course in Windows NT. Jim is intrigued but a bit uncertain. His school does not have a Professional Development Committee and, indeed, he is not aware that the contract for the District Teacher Union allows such decisions about funding to be made by colleagues. He resolves to find out more about this by calling the union. If, indeed, this is an emerging pattern, then Jim is going to file a grievance to get his conference registration reimbursed. He knows that with Carol chairing the conference committee, the registration will more fully reflect the actual costs. This is an expense that Jim feels the district should fund.

Questions

1. What is an Individual Professional Development Plan and how does it work?
2. Should a committee at the school, composed of teaching colleagues, decide how money for Professional Development is spent?

3. Is this concept of shared decision making about funding for Professional Development new? Emerging? The wave of the future?
4. Why would Jim file a grievance over such a trivial issue as conference registration? Is it likely that other school library media specialists in the district are similarly affected?
5. What should Carol do if the superintendent asks her about conference attendance? Should she mention Mickey or just let it go?
6. Is Mickey's behavior appropriate? Isn't it possible that someone will ask about the conference and then the whole issue will come out that she just left?
7. Is it the State Association's concern to worry about what people do who are turned away? Should Carol have cautioned Mickey to go back to school or have just dropped the issue?

CAUGHT IN THE MIDDLE

Gemma and Arturo are on the same team at the Berkley Middle School. Berkley is an urban school, enrolling about 600 students in grades six through eight. Gemma and Arturo are not happy in the middle school. They have secondary certification and although they do hold middle school endorsements, their schools of choice would be high school. Gemma is a science teacher, and Arturo is the English/language arts teacher. Both are on the Gold Team at Berkley. The Gold Team consists of 104 students who came together as sixth-graders. They remain a team for their entire middle-school experience. The four teachers, who teach the core subjects, remain with these students for their entire middle-school time. Gemma and Arturo are but two of the four teachers on the Gold Team. The others are Nancy, who teaches math, and Tootsekahn, who teaches social studies.

Although the four teachers on the Gold Team are considered to be a team, they don't have much in common. Their ages are disparate and their interests dissimilar. Gemma and Tootsekahn are married, while Arturo is divorced. Nancy is just out of graduate school and is still living at home with her parents. In addition to having little in common on a personal level, they are not at all alike in their attitudes toward their students, toward classroom management, and toward expectations.

This past year, Karol Eggers was named the principal at Berkley Middle School. Karol is a graduate of the State University and has spent a number of years as a teacher and as an assistant principal in middle school. He feels that middle-grades education is where it's at. He espouses the Carnegie School's philosophy, as defined in *Turning Points.* He wants his teachers to become team members and has secured a grant to train teachers in working together on a team. He has also released funds from his professional development line to pay teachers to develop thematic units across the curriculum. He knows that this will take time, but Karol feels that it is money well spent. He has a high regard for most of the faculty members and feels that, with some direction, he can turn Berkley Middle School into the best in the state.

Gemma and Arturo are not interested in Karol's initiatives. They continue to work independently, although Nancy and Tootsekahn begin to talk about developing cooperative units. Gemma generally does a biography unit between Thanksgiving and Christmas. The students research a scientist who has had an impact on technology. With all of the emphasis on Y2K, Gemma has developed an impressive list of living and dead scientists who worked with computers. Each student selects one individual to research and must prepare a five- to seven-page report. The report must have a bibliography as well as footnotes. Gemma takes her list of technology stars to the school library media center. She tells Bethany, the school library media specialist, that she wants books to keep in her classroom that will help the students with this project. Because the library media center is on the first floor, next to the office, Gemma doesn't want Karol to be around when she is teaching. She is not good at managing the students in her own classroom and science lab, much less when they are in the library media center. Bethany is not thrilled with having to send the books up to the science room but complies because she is quite busy and would be hard-pressed to fit Gemma and her students in before the Christmas break.

Before, during, and after school in the coming weeks, Gemma's students come independently to the library media center. They want to borrow books on their particular scientist. As Gemma has taken almost all of them to the classroom, Bethany begins to search elsewhere for biographical information. Using a combination of the Internet, assorted CD-ROM products, print and online encyclopedias, and journals, Bethany is able to meet most demands for information. She and the individual students have worked hard to find sources of information about each of the biographees. Each student has at least two different sources and one picture to use for his or her report. Bethany resolves that in the future she will not allow Gemma to handle her assignments by taking materials back to the classroom.

The next week, the same students come back for more information. It seems that *Encarta, Grolier Multimedia, Encyclopedia Americana, World Book,* and even *Encyclopedia of Science and Technology* are not to be permitted for this report. Gemma and Arturo have decided to work jointly on this biography project. Gemma will grade the report for science content and Arturo for English grammar, footnotes, and bibliography. Although the project was well underway before they decided to work together on grading it, Arturo told the students that a proper research paper never uses encyclopedia articles. He further stipulates that if a student uses an encyclopedia, his or her grade will be lowered. Arturo wants the students to do detailed research and find materials from across the state that can be borrowed on interlibrary loan. Gemma and Arturo have placed Bethany and the students in an awkward situation. Bethany ponders what course of action she will take.

Questions

1. How should Bethany handle Arturo's demand for interlibrary loan materials?
2. How should Bethany handle Arturo's requirement that encyclopedia articles not be used and his belief that they do not belong in a "proper research paper"?

3. Did Bethany allow this situation to happen by not insisting that Gemma bring her students to the library to begin their research?
4. If Gemma has classroom-management problems in her science room, is it reasonable to expect that they will spill over into the library media center?
5. Who is responsible for classroom management in the library media center?
6. Is what Arturo and Gemma have concocted an interdisciplinary approach or a thematic unit?
7. Should Bethany bring this situation up to Karol or attempt to settle things among colleagues?

THE SUBSTITUTE EXPERT

The school secretary at the Windy Hill Junior High School is Loretta Ingraham. She has been there for about three years, transferring from an elementary school across the city. Loretta is very personable and extremely competent. She is a good friend of West Pina, the school library media specialist. West arrived at Windy Hill at about the same time as Loretta. Each came from an elementary school, and although they never worked together before, they knew about one another.

Loretta always felt that the school library media specialists were the hardest-working staff members in the building. "First of all," she tells people, "they teach every child in the building. Then, they manage the collection, help the teachers, and create exhibits and contests and whatever else is expected of them." Loretta feels that all of the school library media specialists should have clerical help but knows that with tight budgets, that is not likely to happen. She is always eager to help West, although she feels that he helps her more with her computer problems than she is ever able to help him.

Lately, whenever a class goes on a field trip, the district sends in a substitute. Since there is often nothing for the substitute to do, Loretta sends the person to spend the day helping West. Although this is not really an appropriate placement, it sure beats keeping the substitute in the office, doing filing all day. The principal doesn't mind and West is thrilled. He figures that so far this school year, he has had five full days of help.

West runs a fairly modern school library media center. He has a print collection that is quite up-to-date and is adequately funded. He has been successful in keeping his online catalog up-to-date and now has about eight search stations that also connect to the Web. He operates on a flexible schedule but is so booked on some days that he can barely keep up. He always says, "No good deed is left unpunished." He feels that by creating a positive and viable model of an effective and efficient school library media center, he has created a monster that he must maintain at all costs. Sometimes he longs for a fixed schedule that he can control. West counts on his friendship with Loretta to assist him when he gets stuck running something off and now by getting help from substitute teachers who were sent to the Junior High School in error.

Joseph Sang is sent to Windy Hill on a Thursday just before the February break. Joseph has not done a great deal of substitute teaching and is quite nervous about going to a junior high. He is certified as a secondary English teacher and really wants to be a writer. His parents supported him the last two years while he wrote some short stories and a novella. He stills hopes to be able to make a living as a writer, but for now he decides to use his teaching certificate as a fallback job opportunity. When Joseph arrives at Windy Hill, Loretta tells him that he has been sent in error—they really don't need a substitute, as the teachers and students are on a field trip. Joseph is given a choice—go home and not get paid or stay at Windy Hill in another capacity and still get paid as a substitute. It is up to Joseph.

Joseph elects to help out in the library. West and Joseph spend a few minutes chatting and getting the day laid out. West then has Joseph begin by straightening up the periodicals. Joseph complains about the mess they are in—piles mixed up; out of order by date. West says not to get too crazy about the small stuff—just get the right titles in the right pile and forget about the dates. As long as they are together by title and year, he will be satisfied. Joseph keeps talking about what a mess things are but eventually finishes. Next, West has Joseph work on filing shelflist cards. Although West has an OPAC, or online public access catalog, he still keeps a paper shelflist. Since the library at Windy Hill was automated from the shelflist, he has elected to keep it up-to-date. West says it allows him to keep a handle on the collection by Dewey Decimal Classification number and to keep anecdotal information there as well. Down deep, he knows he should trash it but just can't seem to. When West orders books from a jobber or publisher, he orders MARC records and a shelflist card. When he gets books unprocessed, he makes up a shelflist card himself. Sometimes he has his volunteer help him or students will write them out. Joseph is given about 100 cards to put in numerical order and then file on their sides in the shelflist catalog. West plans to review the filing and turn the cards on their right side. He also has a host of tasks for Joseph to complete as the day progresses. Joseph begins to complain that the cards are too hard to read. He then tells West that he should be more attentive to detail—keeping magazine shelves in order, supervising students writing cards. Perhaps, Joseph suggests, West should type the shelflist cards. Joseph has quite a bit of what he feels is constructive criticism about the Windy Hill School library media center's organization and operation. He shares this with West.

Questions

1. What should West do?
2. Can he really complain about this "gift horse"?
3. Should Loretta be allowed to divert the substitute this way?
4. Has anyone thought to tell Joseph how to behave? What makes him think he is an expert?
5. Why does West keep a shelflist anyway? Aren't there better things for Joseph to do? Should West consider developing a manual for volunteers that would provide samples, standards, and so on?

· 9 ·

Scheduling

HERE HE IS—SUPER LIBRARY MEDIA SPECIALIST!

Michael Duran is the school library media specialist at the Bishop Bosco Elementary School. In this capacity, he has a fixed schedule and sees six classes for library instruction and book selection each day. Each of the classes is for a thirty-minute period. Michael has arbitrarily divided the students at Bishop Bosco into two groups—students in grades kindergarten through second grade are group one and students in grades three through five are group two. He provides two different types of services, depending upon the group. The first group, which Michael calls his primary group, has library generally in the afternoon. The children have a story and an activity one week, alternating with book selection on the other week. During the book-selection week, Michael generally has some type of mini-activity for the children to do while they move around the room in small groups, selecting their materials. This activity is generally related to the story that they heard the previous week. If that is not possible, Michael links the mini-activity to either a story that the teacher has read and used in the classroom or the one that Michael will tell the following week.

Michael has no clerical help but does have an online catalog. He provides little or no instruction in the use of the online catalog for the students in these grades. He does rely heavily on the circulation system to quickly check in and out students' materials. Michael prides himself on knowing the names of all of the primary students. He is fair in assigning tasks to the students—distributing the crayons, calling tables of children to get up to select their books. Sometimes, the children will bring Michael a drawing that they have done. Michael always keeps the drawing and when the class is to return, he posts it on his "special board." The children love Michael and look forward to coming to the library media center. Because they genuinely enjoy their time there, Michael has almost no classroom-management problems. The children are always actively engaged. Michael's approach to his students in grades three though five is a bit different. The upper students, as he calls them, come to library each week, also in thirty-minute time blocks.

Michael has a set of skills that he wants them to acquire by the end of each of the three grade levels. At grade three he wants them to know and be able to use the online catalog to search for materials in the collection by author, title, and subject. He wants them to be able to identify the appropriate source from the catalog and then retrieve it. In grade four, he builds upon this skill by introducing keyword or Boolean searching, along with searching for additional information using the *Children's Magazine Guide.* Generally, each child does a research project and Michael draws in his or her working knowledge of resources to create a meaningful product. He also works with the classroom teacher to reinforce the idea of an outline, a thesis statement, and some form of footnoting and bibliography. Michael tries to tie all of the various instructional strands together with this research project and also uses this as an opportunity to introduce searching on the Internet with several "child-friendly" search engines.

In grade five, Michael continues to build upon the foundation laid in grades three and four. Here, he introduces the use of some specialized reference sources like the almanac, several specialized atlases and dictionaries, and also CD references. He also does considerable work on strategies for searching on the Internet. He spends a great deal of time talking about appropriate "netiquette." Michael feels that when the students leave his library media center at Bishop Bosco, they are well prepared to step into the Information Age.

How does Michael keep all of these classes together? No two classes on the same grade level come in on the same day. Classes are scheduled almost at random during the day, so that Michael may have a first grade followed by a fifth, followed by a kindergarten, and so on. He keeps the shelves in order, maintains the hardware, teaches his classes with enthusiasm, and knows almost every child in the school by name and grade. With no clerical help, he still manages to provide for almost all of the information and recreational needs of students and staff. Here are some of Michael's secrets. For each day of the week, Michael has a different-colored milk crate. Within each crate Michael has a pocket folder for each class that he sees that day. On the outside of each folder he has the number of the class, the grade level, and the teacher's name. If there is a student teacher or teacher's assistant, that person's name also appears on the outside. Within each expansion folder Michael has the following: a roster of students enrolled in that homeroom and on the back of that a seating chart with names of students on it. There is also a note sheet with dates of class meetings already listed on the first column. At the beginning of each class Michael opens the folder flat and leaves it in a prominent spot. He gets the children seated and, by glancing at the folder, can tell quickly what he did last week, where he left off, what table of children got up first to select books, and so on.

He also keeps information about the students—Sally passed out supplies, or Tomas told about his newly acquired kitten so Michael gave him a kitten book. Michael does keep a lesson plan log, but this folder just helps him keep personal tabs on what he and the students are doing. Also, if a child gives him something, he has it available to either hang up in the room on his special bulletin board or it just acts as a reminder that a particular child gave him something. Likewise, a copy of anything that Michael distributes to the class is put into the folder and dated. Michael plans his units at least one month in advance and actually does a yearly plan by grade level. Within his milk crates, he handles the day-to-day stuff, writing next to the date, in his own form of shorthand, what he did during that day. He also leaves himself notes to follow up on.

Questions

1. What are some other shortcuts that Michael can employ?
2. Is this realistic? How can anyone seriously be that organized?
3. How do you think Michael handles his shelving and book returns?
4. Is this scenario feasible, in light of thirty fixed-schedule classes per week and no clerical assistance?
5. If you were Michael, would you find it more profitable to try to move to a flexible schedule than to try to do all of this in a fixed environment?

Chapter 9

AND SHE JUST KEEPS ROLLIN' ALONG

Gabrielle Renata has been the library media specialist at the Williams Middle School for the past eleven years. She has a fixed schedule with very little computerization in her library media center. She does have five Internet drops in the room, and on these she has placed several Windows NT workstations. The school does not yet have a server, but the high-speed line functions in that capacity while the infrastructure is being built. Renata does not let the middle-school students use the Windows NT workstations. She tells the principal and teachers that until there is a server, she cannot protect the students from lurkers who may have inappropriate intentions. The principal, who is pretty savvy when it comes to computers, has tried unsuccessfully to convince her to change her mind. He is optimistic that as soon as the rest of the infrastructure is built, there will be lots of drops and all students will be on the Internet.

Gabrielle is very attentive to her e-mail and spends lots of time reading and responding. She subscribes to several listservs and spends many hours keeping up with their postings. Gabrielle does not have a computer at home, so all of her reading and writing to her net pals is done during the day. She has a fixed schedule of classes—twenty-five per week—and just gives the students a library skills–type of assignment and keeps them busy and in their seats. They are difficult to manage because they are neither excited nor challenged by their assignments. Gabrielle complains a great deal about her teaching load, the caliber of students, her lack of complete computerization, and so on. She is absent many times—especially just before and after a holiday. The principal would love to get rid of her, but she has tenure and he doesn't feel he can justify the time required to document all of her shortcomings. He, too, complains, but the status quo continues.

Gabrielle is on the list to transfer to another opening, and at long last an opening occurs and Gabrielle leaves Williams. She takes a position at the newly opened middle school named North Shore Middle. There, she has plenty of computerization; in fact, the library media center has an adjacent computer lab. The schedule is completely flexible and she has a full-time clerk. The school is a model for computerized instruction and has lots of extras, like the clerical help and the full automation that are funded through grants. The grants have a three-year cycle and then the district will absorb those elements that contribute to the success of the students.

Gabrielle has a rather rocky start at North Shore Middle. The building is not quite completed when the students and teachers arrive. The entire fall semester seems to be a "work in progress." Equipment, furniture, and materials arrive almost daily. The stress on Gabrielle and her clerk is noticeable, and Gabrielle begins to call in sick. The new principal, Horace Economu, notes her absences. Horace is not someone to fool with. He was aware of Gabrielle's reputation but felt that perhaps in a new environment, she would behave more professionally. He calls Gabrielle in to speak with her about her absences and the pattern he has noticed. He tells her that he will be watching and documenting her absences and is prepared to put her on *plans for improvement* (a collective bargaining term for teachers having difficulty) even though she is tenured.

Gabrielle takes Horace's words to heart and her attendance improves. She does, however, begin to leave the building during her lunchtime. She is entitled to a thirty-minute lunch period and to a forty-five minute preparatory period. She has always combined the two periods, giving herself seventy-five minutes off the job on any given day. With the added stress of opening a brand-new library media center, Gabrielle feels that this time out of the building helps her cope. Gabrielle's clerk is entitled to the same amount of time away from the job each day, and both women prefer to take their lunch period in the noon hour. Thus, both the professional and clerical staff are away from the library media center for the seventy-five minutes beginning at noon each day.

Horace begins to hear complaints from teachers and students when they realize that the library media center is locked during this critical hour-and-fifteen-minute period. The students are allowed to leave the lunchroom during their lunch period, and one of the places they may go is the school library media center. Now, this is denied to them. The computers that are housed in the adjacent lab are used by students and teachers for Internet searching and word processing. Since the library media center is locked, so is the lab. Horace is furious. He feels that the instructional day is short enough as it is. Now, for seventy-five minutes access is denied. The faculty and students who complain are also asking for the library media center and the lab to be open before and after school on a scheduled basis. What should he do with Gabrielle now?

Questions

1. Does Gabrielle have the right to close the door during her lunch and unassigned period?
2. What is wrong with the two women taking their lunch periods together?
3. Can the clerk remain in the library with students and without a certified staff member?
4. If this reduces stress and increases attendance, is it a small price to pay?
5. What about opening before and after school? Is that required? Should it be?

FIXED TO BE FLEXIBLE—YOU DO IT

Ashley Barone has worked for ten years at George Johnson Elementary School. George Johnson is the largest school in the district, with an enrollment of 957 students in grades K through six. The building was built at the turn of the century and is huge—three stories high, a large gymnasium at one end, and an auditorium that holds 500 at the other end. The grounds include parking for teachers (there are 78 of them) and several play yards.

Last year, the school added four portable classrooms where there was once a small sandlot for the primary grades. This year, they are converting the unused shower facilities to a Parent Center and a resource room for the math/science instructional guide.

The library media center at George Johnson Elementary is quite large and occupies prime space on the top floor of the building. There is a double door that opens into the center of the room and doors at either end. The space is roughly the size of three classrooms. Not only is it large, it is wide open—there is no workroom, periodical room, or anything like that. All of the high shelving is along the exterior walls, with low book bins and a few low shelving units acting as artificial partitions. There is a coat closet and one walk-in closet where Ashley keeps books on reserve for special projects. Although large, the room is inviting and Ashley has personalized it with posters, good signage, stuffed animals, some rockers, a carpeted story area, and so on. Her principal, Lesley Irwin, is quite proud of the work that Ashley does and does not hesitate to extol her virtues around the district. Ashley is really Lesley's right-hand staff member. There is one assistant principal—a gentleman who is counting the days to retirement and who barely manages to keep the children under control in the lunchroom. Ashley has excellent classroom-management skills and works diligently with the children, teaching them library skills, telling stories, helping them do research, and so on. Ashley also works cooperatively with the teachers, but this is limited.

The down side to Ashley's job as a school library media specialist is that she has a fixed schedule. The other problem is that she is alone in the school library media center. Sometimes, parent volunteers help with circulation, but that is rare. She has no clerk, nor does she have a second school library media specialist, although the state standards mandate one when the enrollment is over 700. The state suffers from a critical lack of certified school library media specialists, so Ashley suffers on alone. Because she has excellent time-management skills, in addition to her other attributes, Ashley is able to combine teaching and circulation within the same forty-five-minute period. She sees the students on alternate weeks and although she enjoys her work immensely, she is thoroughly tired at the end of the day. She is beginning to question her effectiveness and wonders if she will still be able to keep up the pace when she is older.

In her spare time, Ashley is a grant writer. She actually writes for enjoyment and has written numerous grants for both the library media center and for the school as a whole. Because of her grants, George Johnson Elementary boasts a new curtain for the auditorium stage, flags from each country that the students represent, and laptops for the teachers to use while they work at George Johnson. The library media center has numerous computers, CD products, great furniture, air conditioning, and a variety of projection devices.

Each year, Ashley presents Lesley with a plan for a flexible schedule in the library media center. Each year Lesley ignores the request—she needs Ashley to satisfy the contractual unassigned period for the teachers. Lesley feels that her hands are tied—besides which Ashley is doing a great job on a fixed schedule. This year Ashley decides that if she does not get a flexible schedule, she will leave George Johnson. She loves her library media center and her students, but she cannot sustain the grueling pace.

At George Johnson there are already enough special subject teachers to "cover" classes without using the library media specialist. Employed at the school are a full-time music teacher, a full-time art teacher, five physical education teachers, and a full-time science teacher. Because of some of the grants that Lesley has written, George Johnson has over 150 computers. Many computers are located in classroom pods, but 40 are in a lab. Currently, a clerk supervises the lab—installing software, diagnosing printer difficulties, stocking paper, and so on. The faculty is not particularly computer-literate and so, during the budget process, Lesley Irwin successfully campaigns for a computer teacher. This person would take classes in the lab during the teacher-unassigned periods. She would also be available to teach teachers to use the new network. Ashley now makes her pitch to the principal. "I will stay if you put me on a flexible schedule. Now you have the computer lab teacher, and she can be on a fixed schedule."

Questions

1. How will Lesley respond to this ultimatum?
2. Could Ashley have gotten a flexible schedule any other way? Name some ways.
3. Could/should Ashley have made an issue out of George Johnson's noncompliance with the state staffing standards?
4. If Ashley wrote grants for so many things, are there grants she could have written to increase staffing at her school or in the library media center?
5. How will a flexible schedule work with so many children and still only one school library media specialist?

· 10 ·

Physical Plant

MOVING DAY

Claudia had looked forward with great anticipation to this day. As far as she knew, all the plans were in place and the staff was prepared for the great move. Though it looked very simple to anyone viewing from the outside, planning this move of the school library media center in Central School to the new facility in the building's new wing had proved to be quite complicated.

The new library looked beautiful to Claudia as she gazed around the room, right before the move began. The walls were nicely painted, the floor was covered with a wall-to-wall carpet, the new book stacks and furniture were in place, and the outlets for the computers protruded from the floor, ready to be hooked up.

As she walked back to the "old" media center, Claudia was thankful that she had not been in the position that her friend in another school had been: that of having to work around construction materials and workers as her media center was enlarged. In Central School the construction was all new and in a different location than the present media center.

Once back in the soon-to-be former media center, Claudia was joined by Ahmed Salem, the principal of Central School, who greeted the team of volunteers and professional movers sitting on chairs and the window sills. He praised Claudia for her planning and organizational skills and then introduced Gibson Orr, president of the moving company, which specialized in moving libraries. Mr. Orr, along with Claudia, explained the logistics of the move.

Mr. Orr showed the moving team, composed of volunteer parents and members of Claudia's library club, the big portable moving carts that were to be filled with books from the stacks and then reshelved in the new location. His staff would be responsible for loading the moving carts, and some of the volunteers would be responsible for showing the men where to unload the books in the new expanded stack area. Other volunteers could move the furniture and other items that were easily transported on book trucks, leaving the heavy items for the professionals.

This plan of a mix of professionals and volunteers seemed to Claudia to be a good compromise between the volunteers who wanted to be involved and the movers who had the proper equipment to do the work efficiently. There were plans for coffee, juice, and Danish (donated by the school) to help the workers in their tasks and a pizza party later in the afternoon to celebrate the move. Claudia had estimated that the bulk of the operation could be completed in one day, and the moving company had been contracted for that time. The decorations and other smaller items could be moved and then hung at a later date.

Mr. Salem had been apprised of the entire process as Claudia planned it, and he approved of her methodology. He watched her measure the shelves in the former media center and then figure out the needed number of new shelves for ordering, and he thought that she was very thorough. He also was happy with her plans for the new computer technology area that was to be a prominent part of the new media center. Claudia was pleased to have Mr. Salem's support, and she worked on the project along with the volunteers.

When Claudia saw a moving man walk over to her holding a rather decrepit-looking book, she realized in a flash what his question would be: Was it necessary to move books that perhaps did not belong in the collection? She groaned internally and told the man that all the books were to be moved. Weeding the collection would need to be done at a later time.

Questions

1. Should Claudia have conducted a weeding project before the move?
2. Does the rationale of having the professional movers transport the books and the heavy materials seem sensible to you?

3. Should insurance claim coverage considerations have been part of Claudia's reasoning?
4. Is it important to hire professional movers who specialize in moving libraries, rather than general professional movers?

OUR BEAUTIFUL NEW SCHOOL LIBRARY MEDIA CENTER

It was almost a dream come true. Scarlett Agoston had finally received word from the principal, Christian Dai, that the school board had approved the expenditure for a new school library media center. The old facility was so woefully outdated and inadequate that the campaign that Scarlett set up to convince citizens to pass the referendum was overwhelmingly successful. By an 85 percent positive vote, the town supported the idea of a new school library media center that would be larger and would contain expanded services and resources.

Now, step two in the process needed to be faced. In her campaign literature Scarlett had mentioned newer and better but had included very few details of exactly what would be involved. Mr. Dai told Scarlett that the architect whom the board had selected for the project had some experience in building libraries, and that was an encouraging sign. Scarlett asked to meet with the architect and a date was set up. She had heard that the architect would be concerned about how the facility would fit in with the rest of the building but that she was free to make suggestions for the interior of the media center.

Scarlett pulled out the books in her collection that pertained to library facilities and reread the chapters that related to the necessary arrangements of space, equipment, and furniture. She made a list of the items that she considered essential and then a second list of the items that were of slightly less priority. She drew some diagrams of the possible arrangement of the various parts of the center and then decided to make a floor plan with cutouts of furniture, equipment, and specialized areas.

The chart was helpful, but Scarlett found it hard to visualize some of the spatial relationships. Then, she had an idea and spoke to Christian Dai about it. She suggested that she visit other facilities in the area to see how their areas were arranged. Mr. Dai liked the idea and offered to go with her. He thought he might be able to talk to the other principals about costs, dealers, and so on, as well as to see possible layouts.

Scarlett and Christian visited five school library media centers during the month and culled the best ideas from each center. Seeing actual arrangements made visualizing what they wanted for their school so much easier, and at the end of the process they felt comfortable with the plan they worked out with the architect.

While Scarlett and Christian were visiting other schools, the architect worked out a plan of his own for the actual construction process. The site of the new media center was to be right next to the old facility. This meant that it would be noisy during the construction process but that Scarlett could continue to serve the school from the old library while the new was being erected. She could then move into the new facility while the old one was being renovated and made into an integral part of the school library media center.

Step three in Scarlett's plan involved the selection of an automated system and a vendor to implement and service it. She also needed to order new furniture, carpeting, book stacks, and computer stations. The bond money was designed to cover all that, but the specifics of the purchases and implementations had not been thought through before. There was also the question of how to move the collections and present furniture and stacks.

Questions

1. Was Scarlett a good planner? How do you think it should have been done?
2. Do you think that Scarlett really did not expect that the referendum would be passed, and that was the reason she did not plan ahead?
3. Are there considerations that were not in Scarlett's planning?
4. Should a computer system have been selected long ago? Does it appear that Scarlett plans to weed her collection prior to the move and automation? Should she do this?

CLOSE THE LIBRARY MEDIA CENTER— I NEED MORE CLASSROOM SPACE

Betty Chang is the new principal at the Laurel Elementary School. Laurel is a small school with only about 350 students in grades K–5. Laurel is located about one mile from a large elementary school in a poor urban area. Laurel is actually on the border between a large urban city and a moderate-income suburb. Betty was hired as principal because she had extensive experience as an assistant principal in several urban schools. She had gained great administrative experience working there, and the suburb was anxious to hire her because of this.

Betty was hired in mid-July, and a number of decisions about the forthcoming school year had already been made. Betty was told, however, by the superintendent that she needed more classroom space before the start of school. It seemed that two self-contained special needs classes were housed, literally, in large closets. The parent group at Laurel threatened to file an OCR (Office of Civil Rights) Complaint because their special-needs children were being warehoused. Betty was told to close the library media center and divide it into two classrooms.

Being new on the job and new to that community, Betty did exactly as she was told. She wrote a memo to all faculty members, which was mailed to their homes. The memo detailed the closing of the library media center and the opening of the two special education self-contained classrooms. In the memo she also explained how library services would continue, in spite of there being no library media center. According to Betty's memo, the library media center's existing professional collection would be kept in some storage closets that she would purchase and keep in the faculty lounge. The reference collection would be spread around the classrooms, with encyclopedias, almanacs, and atlases given to homerooms in grades three through five and the rest of the material offered to the lower grades; those not wanted would be stored off site. Ellen Suarez, the library media specialist, would continue to meet classes on a fixed schedule. The classes would be held in the cafeteria so as to allow the teachers to remain in their homerooms during library time. Storage closets would be purchased to allow for books from the circulation collection to be housed in the cafeteria. Books would be circulated on days when Ellen was scheduled at Laurel Elementary. The rest of the time, the storage cabinets would be locked. The memo reiterated that this was a temporary move; not more than three years would elapse before temporary classrooms would be acquired and the library media center restored.

Ellen Suarez was only at Laurel part time—three days out of ten. One week she was there for three mornings (Monday, Wednesday, and Friday) and the next week on Tuesday and Thursday afternoons. This type of schedule provided only minimal coverage for services but did meet the current state standards. By closing the library media center, Betty was in violation of the state mandate that requires that each school building have a school library media center. Ellen was horrified when she received the letter informing her of Betty's decision. She was also personally offended because she felt that Betty should at least have contacted her directly, either in person or through a phone call. To receive a form letter such as this about something that she was so closely involved with was just not appropriate.

Ellen did not realize that closing the school library media center was a violation of the state standards. What she did know was that closing the library media center changed her program and was in violation of the existing collective bargaining agreement. She notified the bargaining unit, and it advised her to file a grievance. Ellen did that, but after three months, the superintendent denied the grievance. Ellen was distraught and contacted the state school library association, which told her that the matter would be brought up at the next executive board meeting. Ellen still had another avenue open—she might appeal the superintendent's denial of her grievance to the full school board. She did this but confided to her colleagues in the state association that she was not optimistic. They asked her to submit any documentation regarding the closing of the school library media center. They also asked her to prepare a written statement about the status of library services last year and compare that to this year.

Betty now felt very threatened in her new job. She realized that with the grievance going forward to the full school board, she would have to appear and justify her decision. In reality, she felt that she was forced into her move by the superintendent and the parents. She knew that her career might be over or at least curtailed very soon. She began to try to build a case for Ellen's incompetence.

Indeed, Ellen was having classroom-management problems, conducting library media classes in the cafeteria. The school library association pondered Ellen's situation at its next meeting. The association decided to appeal directly to the commissioner of education in the State Education Department. The commissioner was the senior education officer for the state. Upon notification by the association of the closing of the library media center at Laurel Elementary, the commissioner wrote a letter to the principal and superintendent. In his letter he cited the state requirement for a school library media center. He gave the district sixty days to either reopen the library media center in its former space or to come up with a plan to provide a new and improved library media center in a different but comparable physical space. Upon receiving the letter, the superintendent summoned Betty and Ellen to his office to discuss the matter.

Questions

1. What recourse did Ellen have in this situation?
2. Should Ellen have notified the state school library association before fully exhausting the grievance route?
3. Should Betty have explained the situation personally to Ellen before sending out the general memo to the faculty?
4. Should the state school library association have contacted the school district before going to the commissioner?
5. Should Betty have pursued Ellen's classroom-management difficulties?
6. Should Ellen, Betty, and the superintendent have been aware of the requirement for a school library media center in each school?

CLOSING THE LIBRARY MEDIA CENTER AGAIN!

Ellen Suarez has had a heck of a year. She is a school library media specialist in a suburban district. Last year, at one of her schools the principal tried to close the school library media center. Ellen filed a grievance, looked for a new job, and eventually appealed to her state professional association. The state association was instrumental in getting her principal, Betty Chang, and the superintendent to create new space by consolidating offices. The new space went to house the two new special-needs classrooms, and the library media center was reopened. By the end of the year, Ellen and Betty had developed a real rapport, and Betty used some of her discretionary funds to automate the library media center collection. Although it was a tough year, Ellen is looking forward to the new school year and her automated collection.

Ellen's other school, besides Laurel Elementary, is Willow Elementary. She is there seven days out of ten, as it is a much bigger school. That school has had the same principal and a very stable faculty and student population for the last seven years. Ellen hopes that one day the school will want a full-time school library media specialist, and she is ready. Over the summer, Ellen receives a letter from Thomas Keane, the principal. He tells her that a new teacher has been hired to teach all of the English as a Second Language (ESL) students and that since there is no available classroom space, the library media center will be used for the classroom. In what sounds like déjà vu, the same storage closets that were purchased for Laurel Elementary have been moved to Willow. The circulating collection will be housed in them, in the cafeteria. The custodians are boxing the reference collection for storage off site.

Ellen feels like she is caught in a recurring nightmare. Based upon what she learned last year, Ellen appeals directly to her state professional association again. They immediately notify the Commission of Education, which sends a letter to the superintendent. The letter informs the superintendent that he must reopen the library immediately or face serious consequences. The superintendent ignores the letter and tells Ellen that she had better watch her step—he is considering cutting back further on her hours at Willow Elementary. Ellen is close to retirement and doesn't want to jeopardize her final years' pay and ultimately her retirement pay. She does not encourage the state professional association. She does continue to provide it with updates on her status but doesn't push for any type of resolution. The president of the state professional association is furious that the superintendent ignored the directive from the commissioner of education. She is in touch with him directly on this matter because she feels that in these tight-budget times, this sets an uncomfortable precedent. She and the commissioner decide upon a strategy. They will jointly visit the site and propose an alternative to housing the library media center in the cafeteria, with services provided on a cart. They inform the superintendent that they are coming and tell him the date and time of their visit.

Upon arriving at Willow Elementary, the commissioner and Marsha Odun, the president of the state professional association, meet not only the superintendent but also the principal and the PTO president. Ellen Suarez, the school library media specialist, joins them as well. The six of them meet congenially in the principal's office and then go on a tour of the building. Marsha talks with the parent about the quality of library instruction and the lack of opportunity for free browsing. The parent indicates that she is concerned as well, but she has had to wrestle this concern with the overall impact that the new classroom will have on state test scores. Marsha is confused. She knows that the library media center was closed so that a new classroom could be opened in that same space. She fails to understand the connection between the new classroom and the possible rise in state test scores.

When the parent notices her confusion, she begins to explain. The parent tells Marsha that although "those children are welcome in our building, they do lower the test scores." She goes on explaining how children who do not speak English as their first language require more time from the classroom teacher. This in turn deprives other students of teacher time. Further, when these ESL students are integrated into the main classrooms in the third, fourth, and fifth grades (the grades at which state testing takes place), they do not score well on the state test and thus pull down the averages for the school. This, she continues, has an impact on housing values in the community. Since "those children" do not represent property owners in the community, she supports the superintendent in his decision to open the library media center as an ESL classroom.

Marsha is absolutely speechless. She tells the superintendent and the commissioner that an OCR violation looks probable. The Office of Civil Rights (OCR) will have to be notified immediately, if indeed the ESL students are being "warehoused" for this reason. The superintendent tells Marsha that this is a premature discussion and that they should look at the class currently using the library media center. Upon entering the library media center, Marsha notices children of diverse racial and ethnic backgrounds working quietly at small tables. The principal informs Marsha and the commissioner that they are working in small, cooperative groups.

The children are quiet and on task. The task, however, is coloring pages in a coloring book. Each child has a coloring book and crayons of his or her own. Each book has a single item per page with a single word identifying the item. The books are obviously used to teach the alphabet. For example, children at the first table are coloring the letter D and a picture of a dog. The word *dog* appears at the bottom of the page—in all capital letters. The teacher indicates that the students are learning to pronounce the word and the letter, and that for enjoyment and reinforcement, they get to color the picture. Marsha hears no words being said aloud, and the teacher is simply walking around the room observing the children. There is absolutely no verbal interaction between the teacher and any child or group of children. The children appear to be of different ages—Marsha draws this conclusion based upon their physical sizes. They appear to be at different stages of English-language acquisition, as some are helping others. Not all of the older-appearing children are acting as helpers—some of the older ones are being helped by younger students.

Everyone stands mute in the room—frozen in time and stunned by what is happening. Finally, the group moves slowly out and then tours the rest of the building. Clearly, there is no additional classroom space available at Willow Elementary. Every classroom houses at least twenty students, and no offices are available for conversion. An enclosed loading dock is being used as a storage unit. Lacking heat, ventilation, and two means of entrance and egress, it offers no solution.

After concluding the tour, the commissioner and Marsha exit the facility and walk very slowly to their cars. Marsha is fuming—as an urban library media specialist, she is well aware of OCR regulations as well as state regulations regarding the grouping of English as a Second Language students. She and the commissioner agree to meet later in the week to draft a response to what they have seen. Marsha returns to her school and puts down some thoughts: OCR violation;

inappropriate grouping of ESL students; multi-age grouping; multilingual grouping. She wonders if it is humanly possible that all of the twenty students she saw are at the same level of second-language acquisition. What possible lesson was being delivered in that classroom, with all of the children coloring pages? How on earth would the children learn English if no one in the room was speaking?

Marsha concludes that she will recommend to the commissioner that since Ellen Suarez is only at Willow Elementary seven days out of ten, that on those seven days, the ESL teacher provide services to the students in their main homeroom. They would follow an already established inclusion model for delivery of instruction. The ESL teacher would work closely with the classroom teacher on those seven days. The other three days, the ESL teacher would use the library media center as a place to offer intensive language instruction on a pullout basis. Since there are no provisions to use the library media center when Ellen is at her other school, this will not compromise delivery of the services offered by the library media center. Although Marsha is not happy with this possible solution, it does offer a compromise, and as long as the commissioner agrees that it will be temporary—less than two years until the district can tackle the space situation—she will recommend it to her board.

Questions

1. Should Marsha notify the Office of Civil Rights about this violation?
2. Is the compromise that she is going to recommend to the commissioner reality-based or should she take a harder line?
3. Should something be done about changing the attitude toward "those children" who are receiving ESL instruction?
4. Are there implications here for potential/future school library media specialists in regard to cultural sensitivity and awareness? How about for those currently in a school library media center?
5. Is this an appropriate role for the state professional association?
6. Should Marsha involve members of her board in this recommendation?

III

APPENDICES

Appendix A

ACCESS TO RESOURCES AND SERVICES IN THE SCHOOL LIBRARY MEDIA PROGRAM

An Interpretation of the Library Bill of Rights

The school library media program plays a unique role in promoting intellectual freedom. It serves as a point of voluntary access to information and ideas and as a learning laboratory for students as they acquire critical thinking and problem solving skills needed in a pluralistic society. Although the educational level and program of the school necessarily shapes the resources and services of a school library media program, the principles of the Library Bill of Rights apply equally to all libraries, including school library media programs.

School library media professionals assume a leadership role in promoting the principles of intellectual freedom within the school by providing resources and services that create and sustain an atmosphere of free inquiry. School library media professionals work closely with teachers to integrate instructional activities in classroom units designed to equip students to locate, evaluate, and use a broad range of ideas effectively. Through resources, programming, and educational processes, students and teachers experience the free and robust debate characteristic of a democratic society.

School library media professionals cooperate with other individuals in building collections of resources appropriate to the developmental and maturity levels of students. These collections provide resources which support the curriculum and are consistent with the philosophy, goals, and objectives of the school district. Resources in school library media collections represent diverse points of view on current as well as historical issues.

While English is, by history and tradition, the customary language of the United States, the languages in use in any given community may vary. Schools serving communities in which other languages are used make efforts to accommodate the needs of students for whom English is a second language. To support these efforts, and to ensure equal access to resources and services, the school library media program provides resources which reflect the linguistic pluralism of the community.

Members of the school community involved in the collection development process employ educational criteria to select resources unfettered by their personal, political, social, or religious views. Students and educators served by the school library media program have access to resources and services free of constraints resulting from personal, partisan, or doctrinal disapproval. School library media professionals resist efforts by individuals or groups to define what is appropriate for all students or teachers to read, view, hear, or access via electronic means.

Major barriers between students and resources include but are not limited to: imposing age or grade level restrictions on the use of resources, limiting the use of interlibrary loan and access to electronic information, charging fees for information in specific formats, requiring permission from parents or teachers, establishing restricted shelves or closed collections, and labeling. Policies, procedures, and rules related to the use of resources and services support free and open access to information.

The school board adopts policies that guarantee students access to a broad range of ideas. These include policies on collection development and procedures for the review of resources about which concerns have been raised. Such policies, developed by persons in the school community, provide for a timely and fair hearing and assure that procedures are applied equitably to all expressions of concern. School library media professionals implement district policies and procedures in the school.

—July 12, 2000
Reprinted from the AASL Web site

Appendix B

AASL POSITION PAPER ON INFORMATION LITERACY

To be prepared for a future characterized by change, students must learn to think rationally and creatively, solve problems, manage and retrieve information, and communicate effectively. By mastering information problem-solving skills students will be ready for an information-based society and a technological workplace.

Information literacy is the term being applied to the skills of information problem-solving. The purpose of this position paper is to identify the key elements of information literacy and present a rationale for integrating information literacy into all aspects of the K-12 and post-secondary curriculum. Many aspects of both the school restructuring movement and library media programs relate directly to information literacy and its impact on student learning.

Today, many different groups are helping to define information literacy. For example, information literacy is one of five essential competencies for solid job performance according to the U.S. Department of Labor Secretary's Commission on Achieving Necessary Skills (SCANS). The SCANS report makes the case for developing high-performance skills to support an economy characterized by high skills, high wages, and full employment. A high-skill workforce is also called for in President Clinton's National Technology Policy for America.

Educators are recognizing the importance of information literacy. In 1991, the Association of Supervision and Curriculum Development (ASCD) adopted the following statements:

> Information literacy . . . equips individuals to take advantage of the opportunities inherent in the global information society. In-

formation literacy should be a part of every student's educational experience. ASCD urges schools, colleges, and universities to integrate information literacy programs into learning programs for all students.

ASCD is one of 60 educational associations which have formed the National Forum on Information Literacy (NFIL).

RESTRUCTURING AND INFORMATION LITERACY

Research on the restructuring of schools calls for the teachers role to change from a textbook lecturer to that of a coach. Students become active learners who create their own knowledge after interacting with information from a variety of resources. Learning which results from use of multiple resources is often referred to as *resource-based learning*.

Resource-based learning requires that students are effective users of information regardless of format. Print resources such as books and magazines as well as electronic resources such as computer databases and laser videodiscs will be used by students. Students will master information literacy skills when teachers and library media specialists guide them as they use information with a discipline or through an interdisciplinary project. Another component of restructuring, performance assessment, flows from active resource-based learning. Learning is assessed by observing student demonstrations of ability, knowledge or competencies. In a fully functioning performance assessment setting, student portfolios and other assessment techniques are used to measure outcomes or competencies.

CURRICULUM AND INFORMATION LITERACY

To become effective information users, students must have frequent opportunities to handle all kinds of information. Locating, interpreting, analyzing, synthesizing, evaluating, and communicating information should become a part of every subject across the curriculum. Resource-based learning calls for all members of the educational community to become partners in a shared goal, providing successful learning experiences for all students. Learning environments should be structured to allow students unlimited access to multiple resources in the classroom, the library media center, and beyond the school walls.

The principal, as instructional leader, fosters resource-based learning by providing adequate planning time and budget support. As instructional partners, the classroom teacher and library media specialist are actively involved in identifying the learning needs of the students, developing teaching units, and guiding their progress. The library media specialist facilitates activities which offer meaningful practice in using a variety of information resources.

In an effective information literacy curriculum, the students' experience with information moves away from learning traditional library location skills taught in isolation. Rather, the student learns information literacy skills, as defined in this paper, embedded into the core curriculum. Once acquired, a solid foundation of information literacy skills will prepare students for a lifetime of learning.

LIBRARY MEDIA PROGRAMS

The role of the library media program is to ensure that students and staff are effective users of ideas and information. The library media program supports the curriculum by providing adequate resources, personnel and training so that both students and teachers become independent users of information.

The library media specialist plays a critical role in a schools instructional program. To foster information literacy, the library media specialist:

- Works with the classroom teacher as a partner to plan, design, deliver, and evaluate instruction using a variety of resources and information problem-solving skills.
- Serves as a teacher and consultant in the transition from a textbook centered classroom to a resource-based classroom.
- Provides leadership, expertise and advocacy in the use of technology and resources.

- Partners with teachers to empower students to accept responsibility for their own learning, thereby becoming capable of learning over a lifetime.
- Manages a program (personnel, resources, facility, and services) in which students receive instruction and practice in the use of information. Guidance is given for reading, viewing, and listening so that students can locate resources for both personal enrichment as well as for information problem-solving.

A school library media program that is truly integrated into the schools curriculum is central to helping students master information literacy skills.

> Ultimately, information literate people are those who have learned how to learn. They know how to learn because they know how knowledge is organized, how to find information, and how to use information in such a way that others can learn from them. They are people prepared for lifelong learning, because they can always find the information needed for any task or decision at hand.
>
> —ALA Presidential Committee on Information Literacy

Introduction

The ability to access and use information is necessary for success in school, work and personal life. The following steps represent the basic element in an information literacy curriculum.

I. Defining the Need for Information

The first step in the information problem solving process is to recognize that an information need exists and to define that need. The student will be able to:

A. Recognize different uses of information (i.e., occupational, intellectual, recreational)

B. Place the information needed within a frame of reference (who, what, when, where, how, why)
C. Relate the information needed to prior knowledge
D. Formulate the information problem using a variety of questioning skills (i.e., yes/no, open ended)

II. Initiating the Search Strategy

Once the information problem has been formulated, the student must understand that a plan for searching has to be developed. The student will be able to:

A. Determine what information is needed, often through a series of sub-questions
B. Brainstorm ideas and recognize a variety of visual ways of organize ideas to visualize relationships among them (i.e., webbing, outlining, listing)
C. Select and use a visual organizer appropriate to subject
D. List key words, concepts, subject headings, descriptors
E. Explain the importance of using more than one source of information
F. Identify potential sources of information
G. Identify the criteria for evaluating possible sources (i.e., timeliness, format, appropriateness)

III. Locating the Resources

At the onset of a search a student will recognize the importance of locating information from a variety of sources and accessing specific information found within an individual resource. The student will be able to:

A. Locate print, audiovisual, and computerized resources in the school library media center using catalogs and other bibliographic tools
B. Locate information outside of the school library media center through online databases, interlibrary loan, telephone and facsimile technology

C. Identify and use community information agencies (i.e., public and academic libraries, government offices) to locate additional resources
D. Use people as sources of information through interviews, surveys and letters of inquiry
E. Consult with library media specialists and teachers to assist in identifying sources of information
F. Access specific information within resources by using internal organizers (i.e., indexes, tables of contents, cross references) and electronic search strategies (i.e., keywords, Boolean logic)

Library media specialists help students build positive attitudes toward the use and communication of ideas.

IV. Assessing and Comprehending the Information

Once potentially useful information has been located, the student uses a screening process to determine the usefulness of the information. The student will be able to:

A. Skim and scan for major ideas and keywords to identify relevant information
B. Differentiate between primary and secondary sources
C. Determine the authoritativeness, currentness and reliability of the information
D. Differentiate among fact, opinion, propaganda, point of view, and bias
E. Recognize errors in logic
F. Recognize omissions, if any, in information
G. Classify, group or label the information
H. Recognize interrelationships among concepts
I. Differentiate between cause and effect
J. Identify points of agreement and disagreement among sources
K. Select information in formats most appropriate to the students individual learning style
L. Revise and redefine the information problem if necessary

V. Interpreting the Information

Following an assessment of the information, the student must use the information to solve the particular information problem. The student will be able to:

A. Summarize the information in the students own words; paraphrase or quote important facts and details when necessary for accuracy and clarity
B. Synthesize newly gathered information with previous information
C. Organize and analyze information in a new way
D. Compare information gathered with the original problem and adjust strategies, locate additional information or reexamine information when necessary
E. Draw conclusions based on the information gathered and the students interpretation of it

VI. Communicating the Information

The student must be able to organize and communicate the results of the information problem-solving effort. The student will be able to:

A. Use the search information to identify the important conclusions or resolutions to the problem to be shared with others
B. Decide on a purpose (i.e., to inform, persuade, entertain) for communicating the information and identify the intended audience
C. Choose a format (i.e., written, oral, visual) appropriate for the audience and purpose
D. Create an original product (i.e., speech, research paper, videotape, drama)
E. Provide appropriate documentation (i.e., bibliography) and comply with copyright law

VII. Evaluating the Product and Process

Evaluation is the ability to determine how well the final product resolved the information problem and if the steps taken to reach the desired outcome were appropriate and efficient. Students may evaluate their own work and/or be evaluated by others (i.e., classmates, teachers, library media staff, parents). The student will be able to:

A. Determine the extent to which the conclusions and project met the defined information need and/or satisfied the assignment. (i.e., how well did I do?)
B. Consider if the research question/problem, search strategy, resources, or interpretation should have been expanded, revised or otherwise modified.(i.e., what could/should I have done differently?)
C. Re-assess his/her understanding of the process and identify steps that need further understanding, skill development, or practice (i.e., how can I do better in the future?)

INFORMATION LITERACY IN ACTION

Students practice information literacy in many different ways. In the following scenarios that exemplify cooperative instructional efforts between teachers and library media specialists, students demonstrate their information problem-solving skills through significant learning experiences.

Scenario #1 Three students in the elementary school library media center are working at a multimedia workstation completing a report of interviews with elderly community residents. They are incorporating stories about their community during World War I, photos of some of the community residents, photos of the community from that period of time and a table with community population figures. This report will go into each child's portfolio.

Scenario #2 In the middle school media center students are using electronic mail to work with scientists and other students on the International Arctic Project. Using the Internet, an international electronic communication network, students are sharing data from their own lake study project with students as far away as Russia They are also following an arctic training expedition, questioning and receiving information from the explorers.

Scenario #3 In the high school library media center students are preparing to produce a video news report set in the Civil War. They are searching the school district online catalog, a database of statewide library resources and online historical magazine indexes and a laserdisc of resources from the Library of Congress. Among the resources selected by one student are primary-source newspapers, a videotaped documentary, an audio recording of folk songs, along with books and magazine articles. Electronic mail is used to request some items through interlibrary loan.

Scenario #4 Elementary students who are setting up a freshwater aquarium in their classroom during a study of aquatic life, plan their class time with the teacher before they consult and work with the library media specialist to locate and use print and nonprint sources. They collect the materials, plants, and animals based on their completed research. The teacher and library media specialist locate biological data through the Internet and students confer with the local experts via telephone interview and Internet e-mail.

Scenario #5 A team of middle school teachers and the library media specialist plan a study of life in the middle ages that will involve a special mock celebration. They group students, identify projects that will be completed, and suggest roles each will play in the study. The teachers and library media specialist review the requirements and identify resources necessary, the best information access points for each group, and the most efficient scheduling of time and resource use.

Scenario #6 Advanced high school students involved in an independent study in chemistry are matched with mentors with whom they communicate through telephone and internet. The mentors guide students in projects and suggest sources with which to work. The students negotiate with teachers on the project expectations and completion time. Information needs are formulated with the library media specialist, and materials are collected for completion of projects.

Scenario #7 A district staff development workshop is planned by a team of curriculum personnel, principal, library media specialist and teachers. The workshop emphasis is on critical thinking skills. Information searches are completed in ERIC and other national databases to identify research in the field, people as speakers, and resources for student use. Plans are completed, packets of information collated for distribution, and the workshop sponsored.

Scenario #8 Elementary students involved in a whole language reading program listen to storytellers of folk tales before selecting related books to read. After reading, students advise the teacher and library media specialist on the themes and characters that they think they should pursue. The students, teacher, and library media specialists locate nonprint and other print sources in local and statewide catalogs for further student reading and study. Students use gathered materials for their own storytelling festival.

BIBLIOGRAPHY

American Association of School Librarians and Association for Educational Communications and Technology *Information Power: Building Partnerships for Learning* (Chicago: ALA, 1998).

American Library Association Presidential Committee on Information Literacy: Final Report (Chicago: ALA, 1989).

Eisenberg, Mike, and Bob Berkowitz. *Curriculum Initiative: An Agenda and Strategy for Library Media Programs* (Norwood, N.J.: Ablex, 1988).

Michigan State Board of Education, *Position Paper on Information Processing Skills* (Michigan, 1992).

Restructuring and School Libraries—Special Issue, *NASSP Bulletin,* May, 1991, pp. 1-58.

U.S. Department of Labor, The Secretary's Commission on Achieving Necessary Skills *Learning a Living: A Blueprint for High Performance* (Washington, D.C.: U.S. Government Printing Office, 1992).

Developed by the Wisconsin Educational Media Association and endorsed by the Wisconsin Department of Public Instruction

1993 Copyright Wisconsin Educational Media Association

Reprinted with permission by AASL with additional scenarios by Paula Montgomery. Bibliography revised 1999.

Adopted by the National Forum for Information Literacy, an umbrella group of over 60 organizations.

— Reprinted from the AASL Web site

Appendix C

AASL POSITION STATEMENT ON APPROPRIATE STAFFING FOR SCHOOL LIBRARY MEDIA CENTERS

The success of any school library media program, no matter how well designed, depends ultimately on the quality and number of the personnel responsible for the program. A well-educated and highly motivated professional staff, adequately supported by technical and clerical staff, is critical to the endeavor.

Although staffing patterns are developed to meet local needs, certain basic staffing requirements can be identified. Staffing patterns must reflect the following principles:

1. All students, teachers, and administrators in each school building at all grade levels must have access to a library media program provided by one or more certified library media specialists working full time in the school's library media center.
2. Both professional personnel and support staff are necessary for all library media programs at all grade levels. Each school must employ at least one full-time technical assistant or clerk for each library media specialist. Some programs, facilities, and levels of service will require more than one support staff member for each professional.
3. More than one library media professional is required in many schools. The specific number of additional professional staff is determined by the school's size, number of students and of teachers, facilities, specific library program. A reasonable ratio

of professional staff to teacher and student populations is required in order to provide for the levels of service and library media program development described in *Information Power: Guidelines for School Library Media Programs.*

All school systems must employ a district library media director to provide leadership and direction to the overall library media program. The district director is a member of the administrative staff and serves on committees that determine the criteria and policies for the district's curriculum and instructional programs. The director communicates the goals and needs of both the school and district library media programs to the superintendent, board of education, other district-level personnel, and the community. In this advocacy role, the district library media director advances the concept of the school library media specialist as a partner with teachers and promotes a staffing level that allows the partnership to flourish.

—September 2000
Reprinted from the AASL Web site

Appendix D

AASL POSITION STATEMENT ON FLEXIBLE SCHEDULING

Schools must adopt the educational philosophy that the library media program is fully integrated into the educational program. This integration strengthens the teaching/learning process so that students can develop the vital skills necessary to locate, analyze, evaluate, interpret, and communicate information and ideas. When the library media program is fully integrated into the instructional program of the school, students, teachers, and library media specialists become partners in learning. The library program is an extension of the classroom. Information skills are taught and learned within the context of the classroom curriculum. The wide range of resources, technologies, and services needed to meet students' learning and information needs are readily available in a cost-effective manner.

The integrated library media program philosophy requires that an open schedule must be maintained. Classes cannot be scheduled in the library media center to provide teacher release or preparation time. Students and teachers must be able to come to the center throughout the day to use information sources, to read for pleasure, and to meet and work with other students and teachers.

Planning between the library media specialist and the classroom teacher, which encourages both scheduled and informal visits, is the catalyst that makes this integrated library program work. The teacher brings to the planning process a knowledge of subject content and student needs. The library media specialist contributes a broad knowledge of resources and technology, an understanding of teaching methods, and a wide range of strategies that may be employed to help students learn information skills. Cooperative planning by the teacher and library media specialist integrates information skills and materials into the classroom curriculum and results in the development of assignments that encourage open inquiry.

The responsibility for flexibly scheduled library media programs must be shared by the entire school community.

THE BOARD OF EDUCATION endorses the philosophy that the library program is an integral part of the district's educational program and ensures that flexible scheduling for library media centers is maintained in all buildings and at all levels.

THE DISTRICT ADMINISTRATION supports this philosophy and monitors staff assignments to ensure appropriate staffing levels so that all teachers, including the library media specialists, can fulfill their professional responsibilities.

THE PRINCIPAL creates the appropriate climate within the school by advocating the benefits of flexible scheduling to the faculty, by monitoring scheduling, by ensuring appropriate staffing levels, and by providing joint planning time for classroom teachers and library media specialists.

THE TEACHER uses resource-based instruction and views the library media program as an integral part of that instruction.

THE LIBRARY MEDIA SPECIALIST is knowledgeable about curriculum and classroom activities, and works cooperatively with the classroom teacher to integrate information skills into the curriculum.

—June 1991
Reprinted from the AASL Web site

Appendix E

AASL POSITION STATEMENT ON PREPARATION OF SCHOOL LIBRARY MEDIA SPECIALISTS

School library media specialists have a broad undergraduate education with a liberal arts background and hold a master's degree or equivalent from a program that combines academic and professional preparation in library and information science, education, management, media, communications theory, and technology. The academic program of study includes some directed field experience in a library media program, coordinated by a faculty member in cooperation with an experienced library media specialist. Library media specialists meet state certification requirements for both the library media specialist and professional educator classifications. While there may be many practicing library media specialists who have only an undergraduate degree and whose job performance is outstanding, the master's degree is considered the entry-level degree for the profession.

The graduate degree is earned at colleges and universities whose programs are accredited by appropriate bodies such as the American Library Association (ALA), the National Council for the Accreditation of Teacher Education (NCATE), or state education agencies.

—April 1991
Reprinted from the AASL Web site

Appendix F

POSITION STATEMENT ON RESOURCE BASED INSTRUCTION: ROLE OF THE SCHOOL LIBRARY MEDIA SPECIALIST IN READING DEVELOPMENT

Reading development is a process for attaining literacy by integrating oral and written language experiences into the literature and content areas. Spoken language, reading and writing are learned simultaneously. As students read "real books" and write to communicate, learning becomes relevant, interesting, and motivational and prepares students for life-long learning. Acquisition, organization, and dissemination of resources to support the reading program through the library media center is cost-effective for the entire school district.

The following elements are integral to an effective reading program:

- The library media center is flexibly scheduled so that students and teachers have unlimited physical and intellectual access to a wide range of materials.
- Students are not limited to using only commercially prescribed or teacher-selected materials.
- Students choose from a varied, non-graded collection of materials that reflect their personal interests.
- Students learn to identify, analyze, and synthesize information by using a variety of materials in a variety of formats.
- Multi-disciplinary approaches to teaching and learning are encouraged.

- Teachers and library media specialist cooperatively select materials and collaboratively plan activities that offer students an integrated approach to learning.
- Teachers and library media specialists share responsibility for reading and information literacy instruction. They plan and teach collaboratively based on the needs of the student.
- Continual staff development is critical to reading instruction.
- The responsibility for successful implementation of reading development is shared by the entire school community: teachers, library media specialists, and administrators working together.

—Adopted June 1993; revised July 1999
Reprinted from the AASL Web site

Appendix G

AASL POSITION STATEMENT ON THE ROLE OF THE LIBRARY MEDIA SPECIALIST IN OUTCOMES-BASED EDUCATION

The library media specialist has an essential role in curriculum development. Outcomes-based education is a curriculum practice which establishes clearly defined learner outcomes based on the premise that all students can be successful learners. High expectation outcomes, which are essential for success after graduation, require carefully aligned curriculum, instructional strategies, and performance-based assessment. In their unique roles as information specialist, teacher, and instructional consultant, library media specialists actively participate in both the planning and implementation of outcomes-based education.

As information specialist, the library media specialist working collaboratively with teachers, administrators, and parents:

- provides knowledge of availability and suitability of information resources to support curriculum initiatives;
- engages in the developmental process with the planning team, using knowledge of school curriculum and professional resources;
- facilitates the use of presentation tools in print, technology, and media for dissemination efforts;
- serves as an expert in organizing, synthesizing, and communicating information.

As Teacher:

- determines learning outcomes, including those in information literacy, for all students in the school and/or system;
- plans, implements, and evaluates resource-based learning;
- integrates information literacy into all curriculum outcomes;
- develops ongoing performance-based assessments for determining the achievement of outcomes.

As Instructional Consultant:

- facilitates development of teachers' understanding and implementation of outcomes-based education;
- plans for learning environments supportive of curriculum integration;
- previews and selects resources and technology to accommodate the learning styles and multiple intelligences of students;
- designs and implements a variety of instructional strategies and experiences that engage each student in successful learning.

INFORMATION POWER: GUIDELINES FOR SCHOOL LIBRARY MEDIA PROGRAMS

[This document] states that "the mission of the library media program is to ensure that students and staff are effective users of ideas and information." The school library media specialist is a powerful partner in providing an integrative curriculum that prepares students for success in the twenty-first century.

SCENARIOS OF THE LIBRARY MEDIA SPECIALIST IN OUTCOMES-BASED EDUCATION

Library media specialists actively participate in the planning and implementation of outcomes-based education as information specialists, teachers, and instructional consultants. In the following scenarios, library media specialists demonstrate these essential roles.

THE LIBRARY MEDIA SPECIALIST AS INFORMATION SPECIALIST

Scenario #1—A library media specialist, recently appointed to the school district's new Outcomes-Based Education Committee, returning to the library media center goes "online" to locate information sources on this new curriculum initiative. After assessing the suitability of accumulated resources, the library media specialist selects three full-text articles to copy for the committee members and prepares an annotated bibliography of additional resources.

Scenario #2—A library media specialist, and two other members of the Outcomes-Based Education Committee, are working together to prepare a presentation for a public hearing on the outcomes proposed by the committee. After some discussion, the group decides to use a variety of media to communicate their outcomes proposal. The library media specialist has assembled a number of resources, which can be used for the presentation. Working together, the three teachers select appropriate text, audio, and visuals for their multimedia presentation.

THE LIBRARY MEDIA SPECIALIST AS TEACHER

Scenario #1—A library media specialist, as a member of the K–8 science curriculum writing team, is meeting with the group to identify the information literacy outcomes that will become part of the science curriculum. After reviewing the learning outcomes of the library media department, the team decides to integrate information literacy skills into the study of an estuary. The team asks the library media specialist to work with other team members to prepare suitable examples to be incorporated into the curriculum document.

Scenario #2—A library media specialist and an English teacher are meeting with a class of high school students to evaluate video projects recently completed by the class under the guidance of the library media specialist. The videos are being used as a part of the assessment of an extensive research project on contemporary American authors. Later, the two teachers will meet to discuss and evaluate the process the students used to complete their projects.

THE LIBRARY MEDIA SPECIALIST AS INSTRUCTIONAL CONSULTANT

Scenario #1—A library media specialist is meeting with the middle school social studies department to determine the resources needed for their recently developed "outcomes" curriculum. Suggestions are given for the use of primary sources in several units, and a variety of multimedia programs which "fit" and demonstrate the desired outcomes. Annotated bibliographies of other available resources and examples of assessment products are provided.

Scenario #2—A library media specialist, after reviewing the new curriculum documents and soliciting input from the faculty, meets with the school administrator to discuss the need to provide a wider variety of learning environments within the library media center. A tentative long-range plan has been prepared which would add additional resources, in a wide variety of formats, to the library media collection. In addition, a floor-plan providing more space for production of materials needed for assessment is presented. The administrator, while agreeing in principle with the plan, expresses concern about fiscal constraints; both agree to investigate grant possibilities.

—February 1994
Reprinted from the AASL Web site

Appendix H

AASL POSITION STATEMENT ON THE VALUE OF LIBRARY MEDIA PROGRAMS IN EDUCATION

School library media specialists are an integral part of the total educational team which prepares students to become responsible citizens in a changing global society. In today's information age, an individual's success, even existence, depends largely on the ability to access, evaluate, and utilize information. Library media specialists are leaders in carrying out the school's instructional program through their separate but overlapping roles of information specialist, teacher, and instructional consultant.

The GOALS 2000 challenge our nation to make education a top priority in preparing students to compete in the worldwide marketplace and make informed decisions about problems facing society. To guarantee every young person an equal and effective educational opportunity, officials must provide each school with library media facilities and resources to meet curriculum needs. Officials must also ensure that each school's staff includes library media professionals and support personnel to carry out the mission of the instructional program.

The American Association of School Librarians is committed to the development and improvement of strong library media programs in all schools. The ability to locate and use information in solving problems, expanding ideas, and becoming informed citizens depends on access to adequate library media facilities, appropriate resources, and qualified personnel. Recent studies, such as the *Impact of School Library Media Centers on Academic Achievement*, show a strong positive correlation between library media programs and student achievement.

The American Association of School Librarians urges all administrators, teachers, school board members, parents, and community members to recognize the power of information and the critical need for strong professionally staffed library media programs so all students become effective users of information.

—1993
Reprinted from the AASL Web site

Appendix I

SAMPLE LIBRARY MEDIA SELECTION POLICY

The selection philosophy of the Princely Public Schools' Library Media Centers is to provide a wide range of learning resources at varying levels of difficulty, with diversity of appeal and presentation of different points of view to meet the needs of our community of learners. The Library Media Specialist is charged with providing leadership and expertise—both necessary to assure that the school's library media program is an integral part of the school's instruction program.

It is the belief of Princely Public Schools that no document is final but rather evolutionary. As such, the selection policy that follows will be reviewed and revised periodically.

INTRODUCTION

The selection policy that follows reflects and supports the principles of "Intellectual Freedom," described in the Library Bill of Rights (ALA), "Freedom to Read" (ALA and AAP), "Access to Resources and Services in the School Library Media Program: An Interpretation of the Library Bill of Rights" (AASL), and the "Statement on Intellectual Freedom" (AECT). Copies of these documents may be found at each of the school library media centers in Princely and also in the offices of the district library media supervisor.

This appendix is based upon a document reprinted in the *American Association of School Librarians Electronic Library*, published in Chicago in 1995 by the American Library Association.

OBJECTIVES OF SELECTION

1. Each individual school holds the responsibility for building its collection to meet the needs and interests of its community of learners, including students, faculty, families, and staff.
2. In selecting information resources the library media specialist and the community of learners must consider both the internal holdings and those newly available information services. This is to guarantee that newer forms of technology and information sources be incorporated at the appropriate time and in accordance with curricular needs.
3. Each school is responsible for the selection of materials for the library media collection, by purchase, gift, or local production. The selection of materials follows established Princely Public School Department budget and ordering procedures as well as state and national guidelines.
4. The library media specialist must systematically conduct a needs assessment and evaluate the collection through such means as collection mapping, to assure that resources are selected and removed according to the principles of intellectual freedom. Care must be taken to provide students with access to information that represents diverse points of view in a pluralistic society.

RESPONSIBILITY FOR SELECTION OF LEARNING RESOURCES

The Princely Public School Board delegates the responsibility for the selection of learning resources to the professional staff employed by the school system. The district library media supervisor sets acquisition processes, including ordering procedures and processing of all materials. Collection development planning occurs at the school level.

While selection of learning resources involves many people (library media specialists, teachers, administrators, students, family members, and community persons), the responsibility for coordinating the selection of materials and making the recommendations for purchase rests with the library media specialist and the professional personnel at the building and district levels.

CRITERIA FOR SELECTION

1. Resources shall support and be consistent with the mission and goals of the Princely Public School Department and the aims and objectives of individual schools and specific curricula.
2. Learning resources shall meet high standards of quality in content and presentation.
3. Learning resources shall be appropriate for the subject area and for the age and developmental levels of the intended audience.
4. Learning resources shall have aesthetic, literary, and/or social values.
5. Physical format and appearance of learning resources shall be suitable for their intended use.
6. Learning resources shall be designed to help the community of learners gain an awareness, appreciation, and knowledge of our diverse society.
7. Learning resources shall be designed to motivate students and staff to examine their own attitudes and behaviors so they may comprehend their own duties, responsibilities, rights, and privileges in relationship to the world around them.
8. Learning resources shall be selected for their strengths rather than rejected for their weaknesses.
9. Learning resources shall be selected to promote a balanced collection that should include opposing viewpoints on various issues, beliefs, and practices.

Questions

1. Does this document provide general guidelines for the selection of all materials or just for library materials?
2. Can it be used for both? Why or why not?

3. Are the objectives for the selection of materials clearly stated? How can they be improved?
4. Are the lines of authority and responsibility clearly defined?
5. Do you agree that each school should select/build for their school? If Princely is an urban area, is this cost effective? Should this section speak to cooperative collection development?
6. Although the policy refers to materials in various formats, should there be something specific for online products and searches that are printed out for student use?
7. Are the guidelines for selection and re-evaluation of titles in the existing collection clear? Should they be more specific? Should they be modified? How so?

Appendix J

SAMPLE LIBRARY MEDIA POLICY FOR REEVALUATION OF SELECTED MATERIALS

From time to time, the suitability of particular print and nonprint materials may be questioned. The principles of freedom and professional selection must be adhered to, and the school will have no obligation to remove questioned materials from use before or during a review process. If materials are questioned, the following procedure, based upon the American Library Association's nationally accepted policies, would be followed.

1. The Requester will submit his or her concerns in writing, using the attached form called *A REQUEST FOR RECONSIDERATION OF LIBRARY/MEDIA CENTER MATERIALS*. This form will be available in any of the following locations: the school principal's office, the office of the school library media specialist, the office of the district library media supervisor. Upon receipt of the completed form, the building principal will notify the district library media supervisor, as well as either the assistant superintendent for elementary schools or the assistant superintendent for secondary schools (whichever is most appropriate) of the challenge.
2. A committee of five members appointed by the building principal and his or her designee will then review the questioned material. This committee will be known as the Re-

view Committee and be composed of the following building personnel:

- The library media specialist
- Not more than two teachers
- The principal
- Not more than two parents from the building involved

3. The Review Committee will:

    - Examine the material in its entirety;
    - Read reviews of the challenged material and investigate the acceptance of this material by other professional educators;
    - Judge the material for its strength and value as a whole and not in part, the impact of the entire work often being more important than isolated words, phrases, or incidents; and
    - Submit a written report of its recommendations to the building principal, with copies to the district library media supervisor and the appropriate assistant superintendent.

4. The principal will notify the Requester of the decision of the Review Committee. This will be done in writing within 30 days of receipt of the complaint.
5. If the Requester is not satisfied with the Review Committee's decision, he or she may file a written appeal to the School Board. The School Board will consider the recommendations of the Review Committee and in consultation with the School Board Attorney, render a decision. This decision as to the suitability of the questioned material(s) will be made within 45 days of receiving the request for appeal. The School Board's decision will be the final decision within the Princely Public Schools.

REQUEST FOR RECONSIDERATION OF LIBRARY MEDIA MATERIALS

PRINCELY PUBLIC SCHOOL DEPARTMENT

SCHOOL _____

REQUEST MADE BY _____

STREET ADDRESS _____

CITY/STATE _____ ZIP _____

TELEPHONE _____ REPRESENTING _____

PLEASE CHECK TYPE OF MATERIAL
___ BOOK   ___ PERIODICAL ___ AUDIO CASSETTE
___ RECORD   ___ FILM   ___ VIDEO CASSETTE
___ FILMSTRIP ___ PAMPHLET
___ OTHER (BE SPECIFIC) _____
_____

TITLE _____

AUTHOR _____

PUBLISHER _____

OTHER INFORMATION FROM THE ITEM _____
_____
_____

The following questions are to be answered by the Requester. If sufficient space is not provided, attach additional sheets. Please sign your name and date each of the attachments you supply.

1. DID YOU READ, LISTEN TO, OR VIEW THE ENTIRE WORK?
____ YES   ____ NO.? IF NO, WHICH SECTIONS?
_____

2. TO WHAT IN THE MATERIAL DO YOU OBJECT? BE SPECIFIC, CITING PAGES, FRAMES IN A FILMSTRIP, FILM SEQUENCES, AND SO ON.
_____
_____

3. WHAT DO YOU BELIEVE IS THE THEME OR PURPOSE OF THIS MATERIAL?
_____
_____

4. DO YOU FEEL THERE IS ANYTHING OF VALUE IN THIS MATERIAL?
_____

5. WHAT DO YOU FEEL MIGHT BE THE RESULT OF A STUDENT USING THIS MATERIAL? _____
_____

6. FOR WHAT AGE GROUP WOULD YOU RECOMMEND USING THIS MATERIAL?
_____

7. HAVE YOU HAD THE OPPORTUNITY TO REVIEW THE EVALUATIONS OF THIS MATERIAL BY PROFESSIONAL CRITICS? _____ NO _____YES

8. IF YOU HAVE ANSWERED YES TO NUMBER 7, PLEASE LIST THE REVIEWS YOU HAVE READ.

_____

9. WHAT DO YOU WANT THE SCHOOL TO DO ABOUT THIS WORK?

_____ DO NOT ASSIGN OR RECOMMEND IT TO MY CHILD

_____ WITHDRAW IT FROM ALL STUDENTS

_____ SEND IT BACK TO THE LIBRARY MEDIA SPECIALIST FOR REEVALUATION

_____ OTHER (BE SPECIFIC) _____

_____

10. WHAT WORK OF SIMILAR VALUE, CONTENT, AND FORMAT WOULD YOU SUGGEST TO REPLACE THIS MATERIAL? _____

_____

PLEASE SIGN AND DATE THIS FORM AND RETURN IT TO THE PERSON WHO GAVE IT TO YOU.

_____   _____

YOUR NAME   DATE

Questions

1. Why is the school board attorney involved only at the level of the school board? Is it necessary that this person be involved from the beginning?
2. Should this procedure and the form be available in other languages?
3. By having the Requester submit everything in writing, are they limiting complaints to the more literate members of the community?
4. Should there be a vehicle for interviewing the Requester?
5. Should the deliberations of the Review Committee be open?
6. Should there be an advocate for the Requester who can provide translation service?
7. Should there be a statement made to the Requester prior to the meeting of the Review Committee regarding why this material was added to the collection?

Bibliography

PERIODICALS

The Book Report: The Magazine for Secondary School Library Media and Technology Specialists. Worthington, Ohio: Linworth Publishing.
Library Talk: The Magazine for Elementary School Library Media and Technology Specialists. Worthington, Ohio: Linworth Publishing.
Online-Offline Themes and Resources. Bala Cynwyd, Pa.: Rock Hill Press.
School Library Media Research: The Refereed Research Journal of AASL. Chicago: American Association of School Librarians.
The School Librarian's Workshop. Berkeley Heights, N.J.: Library Learning Resources.
VOYA. Lanham, Md.: Scarecrow Press.
WebFeet: The Internet Traveler's Desk Reference. Bala Cynwyd, Pa.: Rock Hill Press.

BOOKS

Allen, Christine, ed. *Skills for Life: Information Literacy for Grades K–6,* 2d ed. Worthington, Ohio: Linworth Publishing, 1999.
Allen, Christine, and Mary Alice Anderson, eds. *Skills for Life: Information Literacy for Grades 7–12,* 2d ed. Worthington, Ohio: Linworth Publishing, 1999.
American Association of School Librarians. *Information Power: Building Partnerships for Learning.* Chicago: American Library Association, 1998.
American Association of School Librarians and the Association for Educational Communications and Technology. *Information Literacy Standards for Student Learning.* Chicago: American Library Association, 1998.
Anderson, Pauline H. *Planning School Library Media Facilities.* Hamden, Conn.: Library Professional Publications, 1990.

182 Bibliography

Andronik, Catherine M., compiler. *Information Literacy Skills, Grades 7–12,* 3rd ed. Worthington, Ohio: Linworth Publishing, 1999.

Andronik, Catherine M., ed. *School Library Management,* 4th ed. Worthington, Ohio: Linworth Publishing, 1998.

Bard, Therese Bissen. *Student Assistant in the School Library Media Center.* Englewood, Colo.: Libraries Unlimited, 1999.

Baule, Steven M. *Facilities Planning for School Library Media and Technology Centers.* Worthington, Ohio: Linworth Publishing, 1999.

———. *Technology Planning.* Worthington, Ohio: Linworth Publishing, 1997.

Benson, Allen C., and Linda Fodemski. *Connecting Kids and the Internet: A Handbook for Librarians, Teachers, and Parents,* 2d ed. New York: Neal-Schuman, 1999.

Bernstein, Joanne E. *Books to Help Children Cope with Separation and Loss.* New York: Bowker, 1993.

Bodart-Talbut, Joni. *Booktalk 5: More Booktalks for All Ages and Audiences.* New York: Wilson, 1993.

Bradburn, Frances Bryant. *Output Measures for School Library Media Programs.* New York: Neal-Schuman, 1998.

Brown, Jean E., and Elaine C. Stephens. *Exploring Diversity: Literature Themes and Activities for Grades 4–8.* Englewood, Colo.: Libraries Unlimited, 1996.

Burke, John. *IntroNet: A Beginners Guide to Search the Internet.* New York: Neal-Schuman, 1999.

California School Library Association. *From Library Skills to Information Literacy: A Handbook for the 21st Century,* 2d ed. Hi Willow Research and Publishing. Available from: San Jose, Calif.: LMC Source, 1997.

Carlin, M. F. *Understanding Abilities, Disabilities, and Capabilities.* Englewood, Colo.: Libraries Unlimited, 1991.

Cecil, Nancy Lee, and Patricia L. Roberts. *Families in Children's Literature: A Resource Guide, Grades 4–8.* Englewood, Colo.: Libraries Unlimited, 1998.

Coe, Mary Ann. *Integrating Technology into the Curriculum: 1995–96.* Needham Heights, Mass.: Simon & Schuster, 1996.

Cohn, John M., Ann L. Kelsey, and Keith Michael Fiels. *Planning for Automation.* New York: Neal-Schuman, 1997.

Cohn, John M., et al. *Writing and Updating Technology Plans.* New York: Neal-Schuman, 1999.

Constantino, Rebecca, ed. *Literacy, Access and Libraries among the Language Minority Community.* Lanham, Md.: Scarecrow Press, 1998.

Cooke, Alison. *Neal-Schuman Authoritative Guide to Evaluating Information on the Internet.* New York: Neal-Schuman, 1999.

Crane, Beverly. *Teaching with the Internet: Strategies and Models for K–12 Curricula.* New York: Neal-Schuman, 2000.

Craver, Kathleen W. *School Library Media Centers in the 21st Century / Changes and Challenges.* Westport, Conn.: Greenwood Press, 1994.

———. *Teaching Electronic Literacy.* Westport, Conn.: Greenwood Press, 1997.

DeCandido, GraceAnne. *The Internet Searcher's Handbook: Locating Information, People, and Software,* 2d ed. New York: Neal-Schuman, 1999.

Doll, Beth. *Bibliotherapy with Young People: Librarians and Mental Health Professionals Working Together.* Englewood, Colo.: Libraries Unlimited, 1997.

Donham, Jean. *Enhancing Teaching and Learning: A Leadership Guide for School Library Media Specialists.* New York: Neal-Schuman, 1998.

Duncan, Donna, and Laura Lockhart. *I-Search, You Search, We All Learn to Research: A How-to-Do-It Manual for Teaching Elementary School Students to Solve Information Problems.* New York: Neal-Schuman, 2000.

East, Kathy. *Inviting Children's Authors and Illustrators.* New York: Neal-Schuman, 1995.

Eisenberg, Michael B., and Robert E. Berkowitz. *Teaching Information & Technology Skills: The Big 6 in Elementary Schools.* Worthington, Ohio: Linworth Publishing, 1999.

Elias, Maurice. *Social Problem Solving: Interventions in the Schools.* New York: Guilford Press, 1996.

Everhart, Nancy. *Evaluating the School Library Media Center: Analysis, Techniques and Research Practices.* Englewood, Colo.: Libraries Unlimited, 1998.

Farmer, Lesley S. J. *Cooperative Learning Activities in the Library Media Center,* 2d ed. Englewood, Colo.: Libraries Unlimited, 1999.

———. *Training Student Library Staff.* Worthington, Ohio: Linworth Publishing, 1997.

Farmer, Lesley S. J., and Will Fowler. *More Than Information: The Role of the Library Media Center in the Multimedia Classroom.* Worthington, Ohio: Linworth Publishing, 1999.

Fitzpatrick, Kathleen A. *Program Evaluation: Library Media Services.* Schaumburg, Il.: National Study of School Evaluation, 1998.

Gallico, R. P. *Emotional and Behavioral Problems in Children with Learning Disabilities.* Boston: Little, Brown, 1988.

Garrett, Linda J., and JoAnne Moore. *Teaching Library Skills in Middle and High School: A How-to-Do-It Manual.* New York: Neal-Schuman, 1993.

Habich, Elizabeth Chamberlain. *Moving Library Collections: A Management Handbook.* Westport, Conn.: Greenwood Press, 1998.

Haggans, Michael. "14 Ways to Get Better Performance from Your Architect," *School Planning and Management* 37, no. 3 (1998): 24–27.

Hall-Ellis, Sylvia D., et al. *Grantsmanship for Small Libraries and School Library Media Centers.* Englewood, Colo.: Libraries Unlimited, 1999.

Hartzell, Gary N. *Building Influence for the School Librarian.* Worthington, Ohio: Linworth Publishing, 1994.

Hay, Lyn, and James Henri, eds. *The Net Effect: School Library Media Centers and the Internet.* Lanham, Md.: Scarecrow Press, 1999.

Haycock, Ken, ed. *Foundations for Effective School Library Media Programs.* Englewood, Colo.: Libraries Unlimited, 1999.

Horner, C. T. *The Single-Parent Family in Children's Books.* 2nd ed. Metuchen, N.J.: Scarecrow Press, 1988.

Howden, Norman. *Buying and Maintaining Personal Computers: A How-to-Do-It Manual for Librarians.* New York: Neal-Schuman, 2000.

Hurst, Carol Otis. *Open Books: Literature in the Curriculum, Kindergarten through Grade 2.* Worthington, Ohio: Linworth Publishing, 1999.

Hurst, Carol Otis, and Rebecca Otis. *Using Literature in the Middle School Curriculum.* Worthington, Ohio: Linworth Publishing, 1999.

Hurst, Carol Otis, et al. *Curriculum Connections: Picture Books in Grade 3 and up.* Worthington, Ohio: Linworth Publishing, 1999.

Jay, M. Ellen, and Hilda L. Jay. *250+ Activities and Ideas for Developing Literacy Skills.* New York: Neal-Schuman, 1998.

Johnson, Doug. *The Indispensable Librarian: Surviving (and Thriving) in School Media Centers.* Worthington, Ohio: Linworth Publishing, 1997.

Johnson, Doug. *The Indispensable Teacher's Guide to Computer Skills: A Staff Development Guide.* Worthington, Ohio: Linworth Publishing, 1999.

Johnson, Lauri, and Sally Smith. *Dealing with Diversity through Multicultural Fiction.* Chicago: American Library Association, 1993.

Jones, Debra. *Exploring the Internet Using Critical Thinking Skills: A Self-Paced Workbook for Learning to Effectively Use the Internet and Evaluate Online Information.* New York: Neal-Schuman, 1998.

Joyce, Marilyn Z., and Julie I. Tallman. *Making the Writing and Research Connection with the I-Search Process.* New York: Neal-Schuman, 1997.

Jweid, Rosann, and Margaret Risso. *The Library-Classroom Partnership: Teaching Library Media Skills in Middle and Junior High Schools,* 2nd ed. Lanham, Md.: Scarecrow Press, 1998.

Kachel, Debra E. *Collection Assessment and Management for School Libraries.* Westport, Conn.: Greenwood Press, 1997.

Kelly, Melody Specht. *Uncle Sam's Net of Knowledge for Schools.* New York: Neal-Schuman, 1998.

Krause, Eleanor B., and Margaret R. Tassia. *New Games for Information Skills: Ready, Set, Go . . .* Hi Willow Research and Publishing. Available from: San Jose, Calif.: LMC Source, 1996.

Langhorne, Mary Jo, ed. *Developing an Information Literacy Program K–12.* New York: Neal-Schuman, 1998.

Latrobe, Kathy Howard, ed. *The Emerging School Library Media Center: Historical Issues and Perspectives.* Englewood, Colo.: Libraries Unlimited, 1999.

Leonard, Phyllis B. *Clues: Choose, Use, Enjoy, Share: A Model for Educational Enrichment through the School Library Media Center.* Englewood, Colo.: Libraries Unlimited, 1998.

Littlejohn, Carol. *Talk That Book! Booktalks to Promote Reading.* Worthington, Ohio: Linworth Publishing, 1999.

Livo, Norma J. *Who's Afraid . . . Facing Children's Fears with Folktales.* Englewood, Colo.: Libraries Unlimited, 1994.

Loertscher, David V., et al. *Building a School Library Collection Plan: A Beginning Handbook with Internet Assist.* Hi Willow Research and Publishing. Available from: San Jose, Calif.: LMC Source, 1998.

Loertscher, David V. *Collection Mapping in the LMC: Building Library Media Center Collections in the Age of Technology.* Hi Willow Research and Publishing. Available from: San Jose, Calif.: LMC Source, 1996.

———. *Reinvent Your School's Library in the Age of Technology: A Guide for Principals and Superintendents.* Hi Willow Research and Publishing. Available from: San Jose, Calif.: LMC Source, 1999.

———. *Taxonomies of the School Library Media Program,* 2d ed. San Jose, Calif.: LMC Source, 2000.

McArthur, Janice, and Barbara McGuire. *Books on Wheels: Cooperative Learning through Thematic Units.* Englewood, Colo.: Libraries Unlimited, 1998.

McCain, Mary Maude, and Martha Merrill. *Dictionary for School Library Media Specialists.* Englewood, Colo.: Libraries Unlimited, 2000.

MacDonald, Randall M. *The Internet and the School Library Media Specialist: Transforming Traditional Services.* Westport, Conn.: Greenwood Press, 1997.

McDougald, Dana, and Melvin Bowie. *Information Services for Secondary School.* Westport, Conn.: Greenwood Press, 1997.

McElmeel, Sharron L. *The Latest and Greatest Read-Alouds.* Englewood, Colo.: Libraries Unlimited, 1994.

———. *Literature Frameworks: From Apples to Zoos.* Worthington, Ohio: Linworth Publishing, 1997.

———. *Research Strategies for Moving beyond Reporting.* Worthington, Ohio: Linworth Publishing, 1997.

McElmeel, Sharron I., and Carol Smallwood. *World Wide Web Almanac: Making Curriculum Connections for Special Days, Weeks, Months.* Worthington, Ohio: Linworth Publishing, 1999.

Mambretti, Catherine. *Internet Technology for Schools.* Jefferson, N.C.: McFarland, 1999.

Mather, Beck R. *Creating a Local Area Network in the School Library Media Center.* Westport, Conn.: Greenwood Press, 1997.

Minkel, Walter, and Roxanne Hsu Feldman. *Delivering Web Reference Services to Young People.* Chicago: American Library Association, 1998.

Mohr, Carolyn, Dorothy Nixon, and Shirley Vickers. *Books That Heal: A Whole Language Approach.* Englewood, Colo.: Libraries Unlimited, 1991.

More Exciting, Funny, Scary, Short, Different, and Sad Books Kids Like about Animals, Sciences, Sports. Chicago: American Library Association, 1992.

Morris, Betty, John T. Gillespie, and Diana Spirt. *Administering the School Library Media Center.* New Providence, N.J.: Bowker, 1991.

Paling, Stephen. *A Hardware and Software Primer for Librarians: What Your Vendor Forgot to Tell You.* Lanham, Md.: Scarecrow Press, 1999.

Pappas, Marjorie L., et al. *Searching Electronic Resources,* 2d ed. Worthington, Ohio: Linworth Publishing, 1999.

Patrick, Gay D. *Building the Reference Collection: A How-to-Do-It Manual for School and Public Librarians.* New York: Neal-Schuman, 1992.

Peto, Erica I., et al. *Tech Team: Student Technology Assistants in the Elementary and Middle School.* Worthington, Ohio: Linworth Publishing, 1998.

Power Up Your Library: Creating the New School Library Program, by Sheila Salmon, and others. Englewood, Colo.: Libraries Unlimited, 1996.

Prostano, Emanuel T., and Joyce S. Prostano. *The School Library Media Center,* 5th ed. Englewood, Colo.: Libraries Unlimited, 1999.

The Reading Connection: Bringing Parents, Teachers, and Librarians Together. By Elizabeth Knowles and Smith, Martha. Englewood, Colo.: Libraries Unlimited, 1997.

Roach, Catharyn, and JoAnne Moore. *Teaching Library Skills in Grades K through 6: A How-to-Do-It Manual.* New York: Neal-Schuman, 1993.

Roberts, Patricia L. *Multicultural Friendship Stories and Activities for Children Ages 5–14.* Lanham, Md.: Scarecrow Press, 1999.

Ross, Catherine, and Patricia Dewdney. *Communicating Professionally: A How-to-Do-It Manual for Library Applications,* 2d ed. New York: Neal-Schuman, 1998.

Schrock, Kathleen, and Midge Frazel. *Microsoft Publisher for Every Day of the School Year.* Worthington, Ohio: Linworth Publishing, 1999.

Shaw, Marie Keen. *Block Scheduling and Its Impact on the School Library Media Center.* Westport, Conn.: Greenwood Press, 1999.

Smallwood, Carol. *Insider's Guide to School Libraries: Tips and Resources.* Worthington, Ohio: Linworth Publishing, 1997.

Smith, Jane Bandy. *Achieving a Curriculum-Based Library Media Center Program.* Chicago: American Library Association, 1995.

Smith, Mark. *Neal-Schuman Internet Policy Handbook for Libraries.* New York: Neal-Schuman, 1999.

Spitzer, Kathleen L., et al. *Information Literacy: Essential Skills for the Information Age.* Worthington, Ohio: Linworth Publishing, 1999.

Stein, Barbara, and Risa W. Brown. *Running a School Library Media Center: A How-to-Do-It Manual for School and Public Librarians.* New York: Neal-Schuman Publishers, 1992.

Stover, Mark. *Leading the Wired Organization: The Information Professional's Guide to Managing Technological Change.* New York: Neal-Schuman, 1999.

Stripling, Barbara K., ed. *Learning and Libraries in an Information Age.* Englewood, Colo.: Libraries Unlimited, 1999.

Sutter, Lynne and Herman. *Finding the Right Path: Researching Your Way to Discovery.* Worthington, Ohio: Linworth Publishing, 1999.

Thomas, Nancy Pickering. *Information Literacy and Information Skills Instruction: Applying Reaching to Practice in the School Library Media Center.* Englewood, Colo.: Libraries Unlimited, 1999.

Trotta, Marcia. *Special Events Programs in School Library Media Centers.* Westport, Conn.: Greenwood Press, 1997.

Turner, Philip M. *Helping Teachers Teach: A School Library Media Specialist's Role,* 2d ed. Englewood, Colo.: Libraries Unlimited, 1993.

Valauskas, Edward J., and Monica Ertel. *The Internet for Teachers and School Library Media Specialists.* New York: Neal-Schuman, 1996.

Valenza, Joyce Kasman. *Power Tools: 100+ Essential Forms and Presentations for Your School Library Information Program.* Chicago: American Library Association, 1997.

Van Orden, Phyllis. *Selecting Books for the Elementary School Library Media Center: A Complete Guide.* New York: Neal-Schuman, 2000.

Van Vliet, Lucille W. *Media Skills for Middle Schools: Strategies for Library Media Specialists and Teachers,* 2d ed. Englewood, Colo.: Libraries Unlimited, 1999.

West, Mark. *Trust Your Children: Voices against Censorship in Children's Literature,* 2d ed. New York: Neal-Schuman, 1997.

Whole Library Handbook 2, compiled by George M. Eberhart. Chicago: American Library Association, 1995.

Woolls, Blanche. *Ideas for School Library Media Centers: Focus on the Curriculum.* Hi Willow Research and Publishing. Available from: San Jose, Calif.: LMC Source, 1996.

———. *The School Library Media Manager.* Englewood, Colo.: Libraries Unlimited, 1999.

Yesner, Bernice L., and Hilda L. Jay. *Operating and Evaluating School Library Media Programs: A Handbook for Administrators and Librarians.* New York: Neal-Schuman, 1998.

Youth Suicide Prevention: Lessons from Literature. New York: Human Sciences Press, 1989.

Yucht, Alice H. *Flip It! An Information Skills Strategy for Student Researchers.* Worthington, Ohio: Linworth Publishing, 1997.

Zvirin, S. *The Best Years of Their Lives: A Resource Guide for Teenagers in Crisis.* Chicago: American Library Association, 1992.

SOURCES FROM THE INTERNET

American Library Association online is found at http://www.ala.org

Association for Library and Information Science Education is found at: http://www.alise.org

Awesome Library organizes the Web with 14,000 carefully reviewed sources. The address is: http://www.neat-schoolhouse.org

Biographical information is found at: http://www.biography.com

Brian Smith offers a home page on Internet literacy, with many links to search engines, search strategies, and the like. The address is: http://www.cbriansmith.com

CyberGuides are supplementary, standards-based and Web-delivered units of instruction that are centered on core works of literature. The address is: http://www.sdcoe.ca.us/cyberguide.html

ED's Oasis provides links that help in using the Internet for teaching and learning. The address is: http://www.edsoasis.org

Educational Media Association of New Jersey is the AASL Affiliate for that state. The address is: http://www.emanj.org

Gateway to Educational Materials, a special project of ERIC/IT, is found at http://www.thegateway.org

International Association of School Librarianship is found at http://www.hi.is/~anne/iasl.html

Internet School Library Media Center (ISLMC) acts as a gateway to sites of interest to librarians and teachers. The address is: http://falcon.jmu.edu/~ramseyil/index.htm

Journal of Library Link is an online discussion and information forum for librarianship and information management. The address is: http://www.liblink.co.uk

Lance, Keith Curry. "The Impact of School Library Media Centers on Academic Achievement." A nine-page summary of this study is available online. The address is: http://www.ed.gov/databases/ERIC Digests/ed372759.html

Kathy Schrock's Guide for Educators is found at: http://www.discoveryschool.com/schrockguide

Librarians Online Warehouse provides one-stop shopping for library-related products and supplies. The address is: http://libsonline.com

Library Media & PR offers professional resources, techniques, strategies, and communications tools. The address is: http://www.ssdesign.com

Library Science Jeopardy offers an alternative to the game show, with six categories that are specific to librarianship. The address is: http://www.wam.umd.edu/~aubrycp/project/jeopardy.html

Library Spot contains links to reference sites, books, journals, lists, and the like. The address is: http://www.libraryspot.com

LION: Librarians Information Online Network is a professional reference resource for K–12 school librarians. The address is: http://www.libertynet.org/lion

Peter Milbury's School Librarian Web Pages is a collection of Web pages created or maintained by school librarians. The address is: http://www.cusd.chico.k12.ca.us/~pmilbury/lib.html

Reference Desk Online is a great source for facts. The address is: http://www.refdesk.com

Rhode Island Educational Media Association is the RI AASL Affiliate. Their address is: http://www.ri.net/RIEMA

Search Engine Sites

http://www.searchenginewatch.com
http://search-engines.hypermart.net
http://www.howtoweb.com/search

School Library Media Research is the electronic journal of AASL. It is found at http://www.ala.org.aasl/SLMR

School Librarian Emergency Sites has as its purpose a place to present resources for school library media specialists in the performance of their duties and job responsibilities. The address is: http://www.yk.psu/edu/~mer7/soslib.html

School Library Journal online is found at: http://www.slj.com

Teacher's First is a library of K–12 educational resources and lesson plans. The address is: http://www.teachersfirst.com

Term paper help is found at: http://www.researchpaper.com

Track Star highlights a few sites that school librarians may find useful. The address is: http://scrtec.org/track/tracks/s00952.html

Suggested Readings

American Association of School Librarians and Association for Educational Communications and Technology. *Information Power: Guidelines for School Library Media Programs.* Chicago: ALA, 1988.

Lance, Keith Curry, et al. *The Impact of School Library Media Centers on Academic Achievement.* Castle Rock, Colo.: Hi Willow Research & Publishing, 1993.

"Restructuring and School Libraries." (Special Section) *NASSP Bulletin* 75 (May 1991): 1–58. (A Special Section on the School Library for the Nineties). *Phi Delta Kappan* 73 (March 1992): 521–37.

Stripling, Barbara K. *Libraries for the National Education Goals.* Syracuse, N.Y.: ERIC Clearinghouse on Information Resources, Syracuse University, 1992.

WORKS CITED

1. *Encarta.* Redmond, Wash.: Microsoft, 1996.
2. *Infotrac.* Foster City, Calif.: Information Access, 1991.

Index

Absences, 109
Author visits, 72

Behavior, 23, 25
Book fairs, 105
Budget, 65, 87, 89, 92, 114
Building. See Facilities, Planning

Card catalog. See Online catalog
Cataloging, 35, 51
Censorship, 62, 95, 145
Certification, 71, 73, 75, 77, 79, 83, 161, 171
Circulation systems, 4
Collection development, 12, 65, 89, 95, 145, 175
Computers, 51, 53, 55, 57, 59, 87
Cooperation, 71, 75, 79
Counseling, 6, 21, 23

Discipline. See Punishment
Discrimination, 28, 32, 42, 83
Displays, 12, 42
Diversity. See Discrimination
Drugs, 7, 30

Electronic resources, 51, 55, 57, 59, 62, 87
E-Mail, 126

Emergencies. See Drugs, Leak, Liquor, Suicide, Vandalism
Employment, 28, 32, 79, 109
Environmental conditions, 11, 17
Epilepsy, 3
Exhibits. See Displays

Facilities, 131, 133, 135, 137
Field experience. See Supervision
Filters, 87
Funding. See Budget

Grants. See Budget

Hackers. See Vandalism
Harassment, 25, 83, 109
Hiring. See Employment

Instruction, 32, 38, 40, 44, 57, 111, 117, 123, 147, 159
Intellectual freedom. See Collection development
Interlibrary loan. See Cooperation
Internet. See Electronic resources
Interpersonal relationships, 21, 23, 28

Jobs. See Employment

Leak, 11
License. *See* Certification
Liquor, 9

Management. *See* Supervision
Medical issues, 3, 4, 6, 30, 46. *See also* Pregnancy
Mice. *See* Vermin
Moving, 131
Multicultural, 32, 135, 137

Online catalog, 52, 110

Periodicals. *See* Budget, Collection development
Planning, 12, 35, 42, 79, 133
Pregnancy, 6
Professional development, 114, 117
Publicity, 14
Punishment, 40, 44
Purchasing. *See* Budget

Relicensing. *See* Certification

Romance, 21
Rumors, 28

Scheduling, 44, 59, 109, 123, 126, 128, 135, 137, 159
Selection. *See* Collection development
Sharing. *See* Cooperation
Smoking, 30
Staffing. *See* Certification, Substitutes, Volunteers
Student teachers. *See* Supervision
Substitutes, 120
Suicide, 4
Supervision, 30, 57, 71, 73, 109

Unions, 35, 42

Vandalism, 14, 25, 55
Vermin, 17
Volunteers, 71, 131, 157

Water damage. *See* Leak

About the Authors

AMY G. JOB (M.L.S., Rutgers University; M.Ed., Montclair University; Ed.D., Seton Hall University) is a librarian and an instructor and coordinator of the program for educational media specialists at William Paterson University, Wayne, New Jersey. She has received the Distinguished Service Award of the College and University/ACRL New Jersey Section and has published several articles in professional journals and recently authored the New Jersey section of *Exploring the Northeast States Through Literature* (Oryx Press, 1994). She is coauthor of *Reference Work in School Library Media Centers: A Book of Case Studies* (Scarecrow, 1996).

MARYKAY W. SCHNARE (M.B.A., University of Connecticut; M.L.S., the University of Pittsburgh) is the library media specialist for Nathan Bishop Middle School in Providence, Rhode Island. She was 1996 Rhode Island Teacher of the Year and is president-elect of the Rhode Island Educational Media Association. She was named the 1997/98 Milken Family Foundation National Educator. She is coauthor of *Reference Work in School Library Media Centers: A Book of Case Studies* (Scarecrow, 1996).